EVERY PLAY EVERY DAY

MY LIFE AS A
NOTRE DAME WALK-ON

TIMMY O'NEILL

FOREWORD BY REV. THEODORE M. HESBURGH, C.S.C.
INTRODUCTION BY BOB CHMIEL

Expert Publishing, Inc.

Photos courtesy of Michael Bennett, Lighthouse Imaging.

ISBN 13: 978-1-931945-58-5
ISBN 10: 1-931945-58-6

Library of Congress Catalog Number: 2006931928

Printed in the United States of America

First Printing: August 2006

10 09 08 07 06   5 4 3 2 1

Expert Publishing, Inc.
14314 Thrush Street NW,
Andover, MN 55304-3330
ANDOVER,   1-877-755-4966
MINNESOTA   www.ExpertPublishingInc.com

To my immediate family:
Mom, Dad, Michael, Patrick, and Mary Kate.

To my surrogate family: my teammates.
And to Notre Dame, no matter where I go in life,
she will always be the light guiding me.

CONTENTS

CONTENTS

FOREWORD

I felt very humbled and honored when I became Notre Dame's fifteenth president in 1952. In 1987, I retired from my presidential duties ending the longest tenure among active presidents of American institutions of higher learning. During those thirty-five wonderful years I watched Notre Dame change in many significant ways—enrollment more than doubled, the annual operating budget climbed from $9.7 million to $176.6 million, the endowment rose from $9 million to $350 million, and women were admitted to the University for the first time. Change is necessary for progress, but certain things about Our Lady's University will never change. There is a spirit to the place, even if you can't touch it or see it, you can feel it. There truly is only one Notre Dame.

I've traveled all over the world and have been fortunate to hold sixteen presidential appointments over the years including civil rights, peaceful uses of atomic energy, campus unrest, Third World development, and immigration reform. I've met with world leaders, was the chairman of the Rockefeller Foundation, and even hold the Guinness Book world record for most honorary degrees received. Through all of these different things I've poured my heart and time into over the years, I took pride in the fact that I was always first and foremost a priest, saying Mass daily, along with my Breviary and prayers. Out of all the places I've been blessed to see, and of all the things I've been blessed to do, the experiences I regard with the fondest memories are the times spent at the University of Notre Dame being surrounded by students with extraordinary talent and resolve.

When I met Timmy O'Neill he was a senior and had just completed his final football season. He and a friend arrived in my office just as I was about to say my daily Mass with my secretary. The young men introduced themselves and we invited them to join us. We had a Mass, just the four of us, on the thirteenth floor of the library. I am always very welcoming when a student wants to speak with me, and it was a pleasure to have these two in my office to share in the Holy Spirit.

I co-chaired the Knight Commission on Intercollegiate Athletics from 1990 to 1996. The goal of this committee was to preserve the integrity of high-profile intercollegiate athletics as well as the entire institution of higher education. We successfully advocated for presidential control of intercollegiate athletics, rigorous academic standards for athletes, and a certification process requiring athletic departments to prove that they were running fiscally responsible, equitable, and ethical sports programs.

Notre Dame has always been a leader in graduating athletes, and I believe a major reason is the emphasis on acclimating the student-athlete to the rest of the campus. There is no athlete-only housing at Notre Dame, and if you don't go to class, you simply don't play. Notre Dame will always emphasize education first. You are a student-athlete— in that order. Notre Dame will never live with the idea that athletes don't get what they were brought to the University to get most of all. It's not to play sports, but to get an education.

Timmy O'Neill is a great example of this concept. He came to Notre Dame, walked-on to the football team without any promise of playing time, and at the end of his journey, he not only had earned the respect of his teammates and coaches, but earned a full football scholarship—all the while graduating with honors with a major in finance and a minor in theology. I guess he can buy stocks and pray they go up!

Athletics can be instrumental in developing values and qualities often not found in the traditional classroom. *Every Play Every Day* teaches the themes of positive thinking, hard work, and having belief in your abilities. This book is more about not accepting other people's expectations for your life than it is about football. The experiences chronicled in this book truly do apply to everyone.

The journey of a young man or young woman into adulthood is always a fascinating experience, and this book is no exception. It is the story of a boy who decided at a very young age to follow the path to Notre Dame, Indiana. The qualities of Timmy O'Neill mirror the community of the University. Students come together from around the world to participate in enriching their lives and choose Notre Dame to be a part of it. Notre Dame will forever follow this man throughout the journey of his life; just as so many have followed their dreams to the school beside the lakes, under the glow of the Golden Dome.

—*Rev. Theodore M. Hesburgh, C.S.C.*
President Emeritus
University of Notre Dame

ACKNOWLEDGEMENTS

This book was written over a five-year period, and the story started when I was eighteen years old. This book is autobiographical in nature, so consequently, to tell my story, I have to talk about myself. But my intent with this book is not to talk about me; it is to tell a story about a dream, and how Notre Dame gave me the opportunity to live mine. I put my thoughts into words for the possibility, however remote, they will affect someone enough to forge ahead when otherwise they would have quit. The idea behind this book was never self-promotion, it is meant to give a glimpse into a five-year period where I learned dreams really do come true. It is also meant to honor my walk-on teammates who, though their stories and experiences differ from my own, their themes of perseverance and positive thinking are the same. So, if this book elicits a positive response, it is my teammates, coaches, and family who deserve all the credit, not me.

I have always been fascinated with what motivates people. I try to read as much motivational material as I can. That is why many of my friends think I have a quote for every situation and why I have included so many in this book. I've always been curious about what makes one person a go-getter and another person willing to sit back and take what life offers. I have tried to take little pieces of information and advice from as many people as I can and incorporate them into my own life and into this book. We never reach a point where we can stop learning or where a fresh perspective can't benefit us. The saying goes, "Smart people learn from others' mistakes, average people learn from their own mistakes, and dumb asses never learn." I think, at different times in my life, I've fallen into each of these three categories on the learning curve. I think the challenge is to learn from others' mistakes, but there is still something to be said for going through your own challenges and overcoming them. I've been fortunate to be surrounded by friends and family who let me learn some tough lessons on my own, but who also provided a strong foundation so I would never find myself in other difficult situations.

I had the opportunity to hear Warren Buffet, the billionaire value investor and CEO of Berkshire Hathaway, speak when I was a student at Notre Dame. The one thing I remember him saying was that in order to be successful all you have to do is think about the people you most respect in your life and try and emulate them. What qualities do you admire in others? Maybe it's someone's work ethic or how they deal with other people. Maybe it's something only you know about. Whatever the characteristic is, chances are, people are always watching you too, and looking for qualities they deem admirable. The gist of Mr. Buffet's message was to never underestimate your power to influence others, all the while being open to areas in your own life that need improvement. For me, my family is my main source of inspiration. I have been blessed with two wonderful parents and three amazing siblings. Without their influence and guidance I would not be who I am today. For their unwavering support I will be forever grateful.

My coaches reinforced the attitude and discipline my parents tried to instill in me while I was under their care. From my first football coach, Jim Morrow, who took a blank canvas and taught me the game of football, to my high school coach, John Walker, who taught me as much about life as he did about the game, I have been blessed with the passion they brought to their chosen field, and they infused me with a desire to expect more of myself than anyone else ever would. Coach Bob Chmiel, rather than echoing the cultural chorus that insisted something could not be done, listened to my dream and gave me the opportunity of a lifetime when he opened the portal of Notre Dame football and gave me a chance to walk on. Coach Davie allowed me to live my dream, and Coach Willingham embodied character and integrity in everything he did, and inspired me in more ways than he will ever know. To these men, and all my other coaches who sacrificed time with their own families to help me grow, I say, thank you, from the bottom of my heart.

My teammates also inspired me on a daily basis during my five years at Notre Dame. Tommy Lopienski, our starting fullback, had unbelievable self-discipline and an unparalleled work ethic. I would see how hard he worked, and it pushed me to push myself that much harder. He became one of my best friends by the time we graduated. There were many other scholarship players I looked to for guidance and tried to emulate their attitudes and work ethic. Guys like Joey Getherall, a 5' 7" wide receiver with blazing speed, who I never saw give less than 100 percent in a practice or a game. Guys like Bobbie Howard, our starting linebacker who had a knack for making big plays, but was humble and never boasted about his on-field exploits. Or a guy like Chris Yura, my roommate during away games, who could bench press a small country. Rocky Boiman, a defensive end/linebacker, Jeff Faine, a center, and Anthony Denman, our captain and starting linebacker, also were guys I could look at and say, "If I work as hard as they do, good things are going to happen." There were many other scholarship players who inspired me to try and get better every day. Being surrounded by some of the hardest working, best athletes in the country served as both a humbling and motivating force.

While I felt close to all my teammates, there was a special bond among the walk-ons, I think, simply because we knew what the other person was going through. Many of us had opportunities to go to a smaller school where we assuredly would have played more, but we believed in our abilities, and wanted to prove ourselves as football players at the highest level of Division I competition. We all took different routes to get on the team, but the theme was the same—we recruited Notre Dame; Notre Dame didn't recruit us. This book is a tribute to anyone who had an asterisk next to their name in the media guide indicating they were a walk-on. It is a tribute to the unbreakable spirit Notre Dame football gave us, and by some alchemy of change, we were all transformed during our football journey.

I was fortunate to be surrounded by intelligent, disciplined, and mentally strong teammates who embodied positive thinking and the will to get better every day. This was not something I witnessed occasionally, but an ever-present attitude of not underestimating their dreams and what they were capable of doing. That is why I could not have thought of a more appropriate title for this book. *Every Play, Every Day* was more than a slogan; it was a mantra we carried in our hearts every play in practice and every day in the off-season.

PREFACE

*"If you don't have a dream,
how can you have a dream come true?"*

~Jiminy Cricket~

When thinking of a title for this book I almost went with *No, Not Like Rudy*. Inevitably, whenever someone found out I was a walk-on with the Notre Dame football team, they would say, "Oh, like Rudy."

I realize the tale of a Notre Dame football walk-on has been well documented in the movie *Rudy*. The movie helped to put the Notre Dame walk-on in the mind's eye of many fans and moviegoers alike. I met the movie's namesake, Daniel "Rudy" Ruettiger on two occasions. I have tremendous respect for what he accomplished and he is a true testament to the power of hard work and perseverance. With that being said, and I speak on behalf of all of my walk-on teammates, we never endeavored to be the next Rudy. Rather, we constantly tried to fight the stereotype of being the hard worker who did not quite measure up in terms of athletic ability. Our goal as walk-ons was never to only play a minor role without speaking lines. Our goal was to play and contribute.

I enjoyed some of the greatest moments of my life during my time at Notre Dame. I also experienced some of the most frustrating and disappointing moments while there. I fought a constant battle of mind over circumstance and truly believed good things would eventually happen, even when the light at the end of the tunnel seemed a thousand miles away; if I could even see it at all.

In *Paradise Lost,* Milton said, "The mind is its own place and in itself can make a heaven of hell or a hell of heaven." The truth of these words ring so true to me when I reflect on my time at Notre Dame. The world and your circumstance are truly how you envision them. No matter what the reality of the situation was, I always envisioned myself being successful and achieving my dreams. The ability to create my own reality through my attitude is probably the single most important lesson I learned. A positive attitude and a strong work ethic can overcome anything.

But, this book is not the work of Milton; it is simply the story of a journey I embarked on when I was five years old. Notre Dame stuck to my heart then, the same way cotton candy sticks to a little boy's nose. It was during these formative years I first set my sights on playing football at Notre Dame. My parents always encouraged me to dream big dreams, and this was one advantage I had in the pursuit of this goal. I also never entertained the possibility it might not happen. It was one of those things, where deep down, I knew I could do it; I knew I could play football for Notre Dame.

In order to preface this book I think it is important to tell you a little bit about me. I suffer from a quality I call wonderfully delusional. I think there is nothing I cannot accomplish. I believe if I set my mind to something, I can attain it. If I wanted to be president, I believe I could be. If I wanted to travel to outer space or climb Mt. Everest, I think I could do that too! I do not believe we are put on this earth to fail. I truly believe we were created in His image and likeness and engineered for success. It is my sincere belief if people just simply had more confidence in themselves, their lives would be infinitely happier. As Nelson Mandela said in his 1994 inaugural speech:

"Our deepest fear is not that we are inadequate. Our deepest fear is that we are powerful beyond measure. It is our light, not our darkness that most frightens us. We ask ourselves, who am I to be brilliant, gorgeous, talented, fabulous? Actually, who are you not to be? You are a child of God. Your playing small does not serve the world. There is nothing enlightened about shrinking so that other people won't feel insecure around you. We are all meant to shine, as children do."

Somewhere along the way, many people lose sight of their dreams for many reasons. Maybe they experienced an event to discourage them or maybe they grew up and became reasonable. But to me, reasonable can sometimes be another word for pessimistic. If Thomas Edison were reasonable, he never would have invented the light bulb. If 5' 3" basketball player Muggsy Bogues were reasonable, he never would have made it to the NBA. If humans were meant to be reasonable, we never would have invented a space shuttle to fly to the moon or a submarine to explore the ocean. I have never seen a child who was reasonable. When we're young, we dream. Somewhere along the way we lose sight of our goals when we start listening to naysayers and non-believers. We allow regrets to begin to take the place of our dreams, and we start blaming circumstances and happenstance as reasons why we can't reach our goals. I echo the sentiments of what George Bernard Shaw once said, "People are always blaming circumstances for the way things are. I don't believe in circumstances. The people who get on in the world are the people who get out and look for the circumstances they want, and, if they can't find them, make them."

When I ventured to write this book I had a few goals in mind. One, I wanted something tangible to pass down to my future children that is proof dreams really do come true. Two, I think every person has unique life experiences that, if put into words, can benefit others. And lastly, if one person reads this book and is better for reading it, then my goal will have been fulfilled.

I wrote this book because I truly believe in its message. It is a story told on a hundred college football campuses every season. It is about the incredible experience of being a college football walk-on; the joy, the pain, and the raw emotion characterizing the inner fight athletes deal with on a daily basis. It is a journey from the dorm room to the classroom, from the locker room to the training room, and everywhere in between.

In the end, I believe this book tells the story of the triumph of integrity over skepticism. Every person has faced the proverbial fork in the road: *Do I quit, or forge ahead because I believe in myself?* That is the message I tried to convey in this book. I spent five years fighting for an opportunity. This is my story. I hope you enjoy reading it as much as I enjoyed writing it.

INTRODUCTION

When I first met Timmy O'Neill I had already evaluated him on film and been impressed with his high school tape. But when he sat down in my office I was very honest about the rigors of the program. I also informed him that there would be no promises of playing time, suiting up for games, or traveling with the team. A big part of our conversation centered upon the fact that a grant in aid (scholarship) was not to be expected, but that in a few rare cases it did happen.

When I first saw Timmy practice however, my first thought was, "There's no way we'll be able to keep him off the field." His attitude and approach to the game truly was "Every Play Every Day."

I harbor a very special place in my heart for that part of the Notre Dame Football tradition called "The Walk-on Program."

In any major college coaching setting, all position coaches have added responsibilities to which they acquire increased accountability. During my tenure as a coach, I also shared duties that included the organization of recruiting, a liaison to housing, admissions, community relations, the alumni office, its alumni night speaking engagements, and away game pep rallies.

Amidst all of these added responsibilities, Coach Holtz assigned me to oversee the walk-on program. Little did I know at the time, this would become the source of some of my most cherished memories. And in all candor, this assignment brought the most joy allowing for the opportunity to meet and be associated with some of the finest young men in the country.

I had the honor of interviewing starry-eyed high school seniors who had been admitted to Our Lady's School and had a dream. The dream to one day run down that storied tunnel, wear that Gold Helmet, and forever say, "I played football at Notre Dame."

Each year brought a new group, but the dream remained the same. As they matriculated to Notre Dame and went through the process, it was evident that these young guys were a special breed. Their successes are far too many to mention, but, trust me, they are doing well and are members of a fraternity within a fraternity.

Their network is truly almost unbelievable as they stay in touch via their own website as well as at special gatherings. I am flattered and honored to have been blessed in that they have made me a part of their regular communication.

I'd like to explain the process and some of my experiences with Irish walk-ons.

As a matter of policy I was asked to "write up" the walk-on program for Coach Holtz. We determined that the initial qualifications to become a walk-on would include the following:

1. Admission to the university by your own merit.
2. A letter of recommendation from your high school football coach.
3. A game tape from your senior season in high school. And if you were already attending Notre Dame, a clean record that indicated that you had no issues with the student affairs office.

My first question to any young man wishing to become a walk-on at Notre Dame was, "Have you been accepted into the university?"

The NCAA permits a football program to bring 105 players to camp in August. After the first day of school that number is changed to "unlimited." With the NCAA allowing for 85 scholarship players, we were able to bring 20 walk-ons to camp.

Several young men opted to come out for football after the season ended and were then assigned to the off-season conditioning program. The strength and conditioning staff evaluated their efforts as to their ability to make a contribution in spring drills. Spring football has no boundaries in regard to numbers so it was always a great way for an individual to determine his commitment while also allowing the staff to evaluate his ability to perform at the Notre Dame level.

Sitting in staff meetings I was always so proud when one of the assistant coaches singled out one of the walk-ons for a fine performance. Or when Coach Holtz would call me in and say something like, "Bob, call that kid and let him know he is going on scholarship."

I could not get to the phone fast enough. It is very difficult for me to explain the emotion that I experienced in watching one of these young men go from a first day walk-on, not knowing where to line up for stretching, to running out of the tunnel on game day.

But the outcome from the two aforementioned events was the product of hours upon hours of hard work, blood, sweat, and tears. These young men experienced emotional highs and lows while keeping in perspective their true love for Notre Dame.

Add in the fact that this was all done with the reality of likely never seeing the game field, and that these young men and their families financially supported their Notre Dame education totally on their own.

Please stop and reflect upon what I have written and understand why I believe these young men are so very special. Each walk-on has his own story of success and I could probably remember something of each of them. Walk-ons are young men with goals, dreams, and a very personal reason for embarking on this challenge.

I cannot go without sharing a couple of those stories that make Notre Dame football so great. John Shingler was a member of the Naval ROTC, which meant that he not only had the normal obligations of a student athlete, but also the duties and responsibilities of our Naval ROTC Unit. I vividly remember one day just before graduation receiving a call from John. "Coach, do you think it would be possible for me to commissioned and sworn into the Navy on the fifty yard line at the stadium? And would you be there?" I was more than honored to be in attendance, as John Shingler became Ensign John Shingler, United Sates Navy!

One evening after practice I was seated in the South Dining Hall having dinner when one of our walk-ons joined us at the table. As I watched this young man begin to eat I had to stop him because he was about to break the world record for consuming food! "Luigi, how the heck can you eat that way?"

He glanced at his watch, and replied, "Coach, I only have ten minutes to get to my job." He just came off the fields for what was a typical physical, tough Wednesday practice—not to mention a full load of classes and football meetings, and now he was going to work with a few hours of studying later that same night. But that is how you become "Dr. Luigi Rao"!

Timmy O'Neill had some nice runs in Notre Dame Stadium, but it was his spirit and determination that ran him into the hearts of his teammates and Fighting Irish fans.

Every Play Every Day exemplifies the heart of the Notre Dame walk-on and embodies the sprit I felt while overseeing the "Walk-on Program" at Notre Dame. The story that follows captures one of the most unique Notre Dame experiences with a tradition and camaraderie unlike any other.

When a young man puts on that gold helmet it makes no difference how he arrived at the honor. He wears it proudly because he is a Notre Dame man!

~Coach Bob Chmiel~

walk-on (wôk´ŏn´, -ôn´) *n.*

1. A minor role, usually without speaking lines.
2. A performer playing such a role.

~The American Heritage® Dictionary of the English Language, Fourth Edition © 2000 by Houghton Mifflin Company~

COMMITMENT

Commitment is what transforms a promise into reality.
It is the words that speak boldly of your intentions.
And the actions which speak louder than words.
Commitment is making the time when there is none.
Coming through time after time, year after year.
It has the power to change the face of things.
It is the daily triumph of integrity over skepticism.

~Quote from Notre Dame's weight room~

ONE

DREAMERS

"Nothing happens, unless first a dream."

~Carl Sandberg~

otre Dame's original dreamer was Father Edward Sorin, a member of a small group of priests and brothers known as the Congregation of the Holy Cross, who founded the University in 1842. Father Sorin's vision for the University is best exemplified in a letter he wrote that same year. He stated, "...this college cannot fail to succeed...Before long it will develop on a large scale...It will be one of the most powerful means for good in this country." The school was founded as a mission station on two small lakes north of South Bend, Indiana, near the St. Joseph River. Sorin saw the frozen lakes with their mantles of new white snow as a symbol of the purity of Our Lady. That is why this mission station by the lakes forever would come to be known as Notre Dame du Lac (Our Lady by the Lake).

But more than simply providing a charter and a plot of land for the University, Father Sorin provided a faith and resilience that permeated the University and gave it a tradition and legacy of triumph. He named the school after the mother of Jesus, and even before the first buildings were completed, said, "When this school, Our Lady's school, grows a bit more, I shall raise her aloft so that, without asking, [all] men shall forever know why we have succeeded here. To that lovely Lady, raised high on a dome, men may look and find the answer." This building would eventually be built as Father Sorin promised, but on April 23, 1879, the main building was engulfed in flames and the dome and roof collapsed as the fire spread to other buildings.

The same day Father Sorin looked at the ashes of his dream laid out in the glowing rubble, he motioned his followers into the church, which miraculously was not harmed by the flames. Once inside, he said to his downtrodden followers who were quickly losing faith, "The fire has been my fault, I came here with the vision of a great university and named it after the mother of Jesus. Then we built a large university, or so I thought. But she had to burn it to the ground to show me that my vision was too narrow and that I had dreamed too small a dream." Father Sorin continued, "Tomorrow when the bricks are cooled, we will clean them and begin again. This time we will build a really large building and when it is built we will put a gold dome on the top and we will crown it with a golden statue of Mary, the mother of our Lord Jesus Christ, so that everyone who comes this way will know to whom we owe whatever great future God has planned for this university of ours. Even if it were all destroyed again, I shall never give up." This golden dome Father Sorin envisioned, even as the smoke was still wafting to the heavens less than a hundred feet from where he made his proclamation, is now one of the most recognizable campus landmarks in the world.

This spirit of never giving up and dreaming big dreams is the heart and soul of the University and the reason it has developed such a following and a reputation for overcoming seemingly insurmountable odds. At its heart, Notre Dame is a Catholic institution committed to building a community of faith among its students and faculty to better serve society and the world. But no other institutions' roots are so entwined and synonymous with a sport. Notre Dame is so much more than football; its soul is steadfastly committed to service through faith and action, but without football, it would never be the national institution it is today.

In 1918, Notre Dame hired a young, inexperienced coach named Knute Rockne, who laid the framework for a football tradition unparalleled in college athletics. In the early 1920s, a period that came to be known as the Golden Age of Sports, the national sports media began to take notice of the small Midwestern school in South Bend, Indiana. In the years following the end of World War I, intercollegiate football experienced an explosion in popularity and Notre Dame found itself at the heart of this new American machine. Rockne was as well known a public figure as there was in his day, producing more championship teams and all-American players than any coach of his generation. Rockne had a gift for promotion, and he knew how to use the media to promulgate the University's interests to the masses.

Rockne catapulted Notre Dame into the national consciousness propelling the game of football from the traditional closed style of play to a more open style of football, emphasizing quickness and deception. He is credited with inventing the forward pass, and his locker room speeches are the stuff of legend. Tragically, the life of this charismatic coach was cut short at the age of forty-three when a plane carrying Rockne and seven other passengers crashed in Bazaar, Kansas. His death shocked the country and his funeral was broadcast live to Europe, South America, and Asia. In his tenure at the helm of the Notre Dame football program he established a tradition and a following that lives on today in the hearts and minds of millions of fans across the country and throughout the world.

The next great Notre Dame coach following Rockne was Frank Leahy. Leahy coached the Irish for eleven seasons from 1941 to 1943 and from 1946 to 1953. His footprint on the college football landscape is firmly imprinted with the second highest winning percentage (86.4 percent) of any college coach in history. He led the Irish to a record of eighty-seven wins, eleven losses, and nine ties including thirty-nine games without a loss (37-0-2), four national championships, and six undefeated seasons.

The "Era of Ara," began in 1964 when Ara Parseghian accepted the head coaching job after an eight-year stint at Northwestern University. He coached Notre Dame from 1964–1974, and, during his eleven-year career, compiled a record of ninety-five wins, seventeen losses, and four ties, en route to capturing two uncontested national championships.

Dan Devine and Lou Holtz would each add a national championship to their coaching resumes in 1977 and 1988, respectively, giving Notre Dame more national championships than any other school in college football history.

The seeds Rockne, Leahy, Parseghian, Devine, and Holtz planted were firmly rooted when I attended my first Notre Dame football game.

I was seven years old, and I guess my dad thought the time had come to indoctrinate me. There is a special connection between a boy and his dad, which can be magnified through sports. Everything about that fall afternoon struck a chord in me that resonated throughout my childhood. Football Saturdays have a rich tradition in the lexicon of college football, but at Notre Dame, a football Saturday is a religious experience.

When I was growing up, going to a Notre Dame football game was an annual pilgrimage, like going to Mecca, or Lourdes, or Jerusalem. When I attended my first Notre Dame game, I experienced something visceral. I felt an esoteric camaraderie and the feeling was not something I could package together and bring home to show my friends. It was something that transcended the present moment, and I could feel it, even though I could not see it. For brief moments on those fall afternoons I was part of the tradition, a part of the history. It took only one of these awe-inspiring trips to campus for me to know Notre Dame would always be a part of me—and would be the place I would play football one day.

The magic begins long before kickoff. My first Notre Dame game was the 1987 Notre Dame versus Michigan State game, which is still one of only a handful of night games ever played in Notre Dame stadium. My dad took me to the game, but before taking me, he faced a moral dilemma. He had tickets to see the pope in Detroit, but he also had tickets to the Notre Dame game. In the end, he took me to the Notre Dame game because he thought it would be more of a religious experience for me! It's a wonder we weren't struck by lighting in the car ride to South Bend, Indiana.

The night before every home football game there is a pep rally. My dad took me to this standing-room-only event the night before Notre Dame played Michigan State. The pep rally begins at 7:00 p.m. and includes performances by the band, the cheerleaders, and the dance team. After the performances there is usually a celebrity speaker, followed by speeches from two football players, and then, lastly, the head coach addresses the congregation. For a seven-year-old, the site of one hundred Notre Dame football players dressed in suits being supported by twelve thousand loyal fans left a lasting impression.

After the pep rally we walked over to the stadium and witnessed another Friday night ritual. Before every game, home and away, the football managers paint each player's helmet gold, using paint containing real gold dust. Hundreds of spectators gather behind the gates at the north side of the stadium to witness a tradition that has been in place since the mid-1960s. Perhaps it was the paint fumes I inhaled standing behind the gates watching the helmets glisten, but I had no doubt, even at age seven, someday the managers would be painting a helmet belonging to me.

The next morning my dad woke me up early so we could take in the sites and sounds of the campus on game day. The campus usually comes alive at 7:00 a.m. when the students wake up to begin the day's festivities. But since this was a night game the students slept in on this particular Saturday. Still, throughout the day the campus was besieged with fans of all kinds, from the little girl in pig tails wearing the Notre Dame cheerleading uniform, to the 1932 graduate who looks like he dressed in the dark wearing his collage of Notre Dame colors as a visual reminder of his heart's allegiance. Notre Dame's campus landmarks become a pilgrimage for some on game day. The Grotto, the Basilica of the Sacred Heart, the Golden Dome, and the Hesburgh Library, with its famous façade colloquially known as Touchdown Jesus, receive thousands of visitors on these fall afternoons.

But our destination that day was Bond Hall, the architecture building where the band congregates before raising their cacophony of sound throughout their marching tour of campus. I watched and listened as the brainwashing continued. This time the vehicle of manipulation came in the form of music. Once I heard the fight song (whose words I already memorized), I was forever hooked on the Notre Dame mystique. I began to get goose bumps. From the steps of Bond Hall we followed the band on their march to the stadium. In their wake they left a line of people four or five deep on either side of the walkway. Upon reaching the stadium the band filed in through the main gate, and my dad and I made our way to our seats.

Chants of "LET'S GO IRISH!" greeted us as we navigated to our seats. At the time of my maiden voyage into Notre Dame Stadium, it only seated fifty-nine thousand. The stadium has since been renovated and now houses over eighty thousand. In this intimate stadium environment the "LET'S GO IRISH!" chant reached a crescendo by the time we found our seats on the forty-yard line, four rows from the top of the stadium. My dad and I secured a perfect vantage point for the events about to transpire.

A hush filled the stadium as the Notre Dame team began to form a bottleneck in the tunnel at the north end of the stadium. First, I could see only one gold helmet, then two, and then a dozen, then the entire team was bouncing together in a mass of excited energy. To me, they were gladiators, invincible machines ready to annihilate anything in their path. By this time I had joined in the chorus of another chant, "HERE COME THE IRISH! HERE COME THE IRISH!" As if beckoning to the call of the stadium, Notre Dame's head coach, Lou Holtz, gave the signal to move and the team charged out of the tunnel and onto the freshly manicured field.

The game offered everything I could have dreamed and exceeded every expectation a bright-eyed seven-year-old could have. Notre Dame had a senior speedster out of Dallas, Texas, who many considered to be the best player in the country. His name was Tim Brown and he played flanker, was used as a running back in certain formations, and was also a dynamic kickoff and punt returner. On that crisp September night in 1987, I watched Tim Brown stake his claim on the most coveted award in college football—the Heisman Trophy. On that night, against a Michigan State team who would eventually be crowned Big Ten and Rose Bowl champions, he had back-to-back punt returns for touchdowns. His runs of sixty-six and seventy-one yards solidified his position among college football's best players. At the end of the season, Tim Brown became Notre Dame's seventh Heisman Trophy winner, due in large part to his performance against Michigan State. The excitement in the stadium was electric, and I knew I wanted to be a part of the emotion one day.

After my initial foray into the Notre Dame experience, I went home and wrote a letter to my new hero. It read, errors and all,

Dear Timmy Brown,

Yesterday my daddy took me to the Notre Dame vs. Michigan State game. I saw you run back too touchdowns. I'm seven years old and I like football and I think you are grate. I would be so happy if you would sign your name on this paper and send it back to me to show my friends.

Your friend,
Timmy O'Neill

Six months later I received a letter postmarked from Dallas, Texas, Tim Brown's hometown. He had signed it, "Best Wishes, Tim Brown #81." I was awed. Tim Brown had taken the time to respond to my letter. It was a feeling I would remember fifteen years later when I found myself on the receiving end of a similar letter.

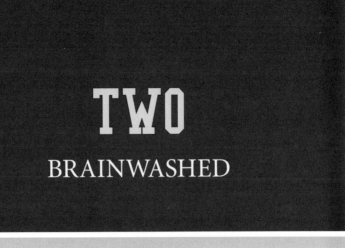

TWO

BRAINWASHED

"We choose those we like; with those we love, we have no say in the matter."

~Mignon McLaughlin, *The Neurotic's Notebook*, 1960~

To understand my love for Notre Dame is to understand how I grew up. While most little boys were learning their multiplication tables and how to pen a capital Q in cursive, I was also memorizing the names of the Four Horsemen and George Gipp's last words. I knew more about Notre Dame by the time I was seven years old than most graduates of other universities ever know about their alma mater. When I was little I not only wore the interlocking ND on my T-shirts, but I also had Notre Dame in my blood, and I was willing to fight anyone who disrespected the school I loved. On one such occasion, the assistant principal called my dad to pick me up from school after I got into a fight. I sat in the car with trembling knees, not knowing what my dad's reaction would be to my transgression. The first thing he said during the ride home after five minutes of silence was, "Did you win?" He then told me I couldn't force someone to love Notre Dame who didn't want to open their heart to the magic. There would be no more in-school fights for me—at least not because of Notre Dame.

There was one constant thing in my life while I was growing up. I was always thinking about Notre Dame football. Before I went to bed at night I visualized myself running through the tunnel. When I said my prayers, I always ended them with, "If it is your will, dear Lord, let me play football for Notre Dame." When my teachers asked me to write short stories when I was in elementary school, my stories, more often than not, revolved around three key plot points: Notre Dame, football, and me.

My teachers would say to me, "Timmy, you have to start writing about something else."

And I would reply, "But that's the only thing that interests me."

I think every Notre Dame alumni takes Brainwashing 101 as a prerequisite to graduate. I learned at a very young age Notre Dame is a special place. If it was a Saturday in the fall, all eyes in my household stared at the gold helmets dotting the television set. As far back as my memory allows me to travel, I have loved Notre Dame and its storied football tradition. There was never a time in my life when those two things were not important to me: football and Notre Dame. In my mind, those two terms will never be mutually exclusive. My experiences growing up in what I call the "Notre Dame culture" are not unique. There are thousands of children who grow up in a similar way. The Notre Dame lore and tradition is indoctrinated at an early age when we are young and malleable. That is why we love Notre Dame. That is also why many hate Notre Dame.

I come from a long line of Notre Dame graduates. My oldest brother, Michael, and I were the fourth generation of my family to attend Notre Dame. My father graduated in 1961, my grandfather graduated in 1926, and my great-grandfather graduated in 1906. Two of my uncles also attended Notre Dame, as well as my great-aunt who was a nun. She earned her degree while attending only summer classes, because at that time Notre Dame did not admit women. With all my relatives that attended Notre Dame, we could have started our own alumni club. It was not until I was older that I came to understand my family's tradition with the university. To me, all that mattered when I was younger was how excited I saw my dad get when the Notre Dame football team scored. And how I had to duck for cover when they didn't.

My great-grandfather, William P. O'Neill, grew up in Mishawaka, Indiana, the neighboring town next to South Bend. When he was growing up, Notre Dame also had a grade school, and he served as an altar boy for Father Sorin. My great-grandfather attended Notre Dame from 1887 to 1890, before he left to get married and raise his five children. He later returned to Notre Dame and graduated with a law degree in 1906. He used to ride his horse to campus from his home in Mishawaka and hitch it to the main building while he attended classes. My great-grandfather was later elected the Lieutenant Governor of the state of Indiana, and served in that capacity from 1913–1917.

My grandfather, Dennis O'Neill, attended Notre Dame from 1922-1926. During his time at Notre Dame, he was editor of the 1926 yearbook; class poet (they had one in those days); editor of the *Scribbler*, a literary magazine; and a regular contributor to poetry publications. The famous poet Carl Sandburg was even on his board of advisors for one of his publications. Upon graduation, my grandfather became a published author and poet and was the vice president of D'arcy Advertising.

I think I get my love of writing from my grandfather. However, his success in winning over the ladies with his poetry have garnered him far greater results than my own. My grandmother eventually succumbed to his advances, in no small part because of his talent with prose. Consequently, in 1927, with soon-to-be-named university president Father Charles O'Donnell presiding, my grandparents, Dennis and Dorothy O'Neill, were married on campus in the log chapel. Notre Dame's log chapel was completed in 1906 after the original log chapel burned down in 1856. It is one of the oldest campus landmarks and represents the very beginnings of the university.

My father graduated in 1961 and claims to have made the dean's list the second semester of his junior year. This claim, however, had not yet been validated at the time this book went to print. My parents, F. Michael and Karen O'Neill, were also married on campus in the Basilica of the Sacred Heart. Ten years after their day of celebration, they had increased their number three-fold. Michael, my oldest brother was first, followed by Patrick, Mary Kate, and last, but not least, me.

My oldest brother, Michael, graduated from Notre Dame in 1992. He walked on to the football team the spring of his sophomore year. He tied for the highest vertical on the team with all-American running back Reggie Brooks. Michael was awarded the game ball for the Navy game from Coach Holtz for his performance during the preceding week of practice. When Coach Holtz presented Michael with the game ball, he was on one knee behind the starting quarterback (and eventual first round draft pick, Rick Mirer). Coach Holtz had to call my brother's name twice before my brother realized he was talking to him.

Holtz, in his witty style that had become his trademark, told my brother before giving him the game ball, "Sorry, Mike, I didn't see you back there; Rick Mirer's ego got in the way."

The first game I went to when Michael played on the team was against Michigan State. My brother played fullback and went into the game on an "Iso" play. In football parlance, an "Iso" play is where the fullback is isolated against the linebacker. The fullback's only job on this play is to eliminate the linebacker. And Michael did, paving the way for a twenty-yard gain for the tailback.

I was shouting in the stands, "That's my bro!"

My other brother, Patrick, played football at Western Michigan. He was also a walk-on. He was one of the strongest members on the team despite only weighing 165 pounds. He could bench press 225 pounds, twenty-eight times.

My sister, Mary Kate, was also an excellent athlete. In high school, she was a member of a state championship soccer team.

All of my siblings served as motivation for me and were constant reminders of the limits you can push your body to with hard work. Because both of my brothers experienced college football, they helped pave the way for me by providing first-hand advice on the life of a Division I college football player and what it took to be successful. They gave me confidence the people they were competing with every day were their equals and not people of which to be in awe.

After attending my first game when I was seven years old with my dad, seeing a Notre Dame Football game became an annual pilgrimage. On one such occasion, when I was in fourth grade, I was staying at the Holiday Inn in South Bend with my parents. At breakfast, we noticed a man wearing a Ricky Watters button, and a #12 jersey. Ricky Watters was an all-American tailback during the Lou Holtz era. Watters went on to NFL fame with the San Francisco 49ers and Seattle Seahawks. From all outward appearances this man had to be his father. We struck up a conversation with him and our assumption proved correct. Of course, we talked football. As I was in fourth grade, I had not started playing yet, but I kept bugging my mom to let me partake in full padded football.

So my mom asked Ricky Watter's father, "When should Timmy start?"

He looked at me, then at her, and said, "What grade is he in?"

My mom informed him of my fourth grade status, and he said, "It's already too late."

I had already wasted too much time—my biological clock was ticking. Mr. Watter's told us stories of how Ricky used to play tackle on the pavement with the older kids when he was growing up. These Notre Dame players were tough! I had a ways to go before I could reach my goals. So on the advice of Ricky Watters' father, my football career started the following fall.

I dabbled in every sport throughout my younger years. They gave me self-confidence and helped cultivate lasting friendships I otherwise would have missed. I speak with certainty that my participation in athletics has taught me more about life than any classroom could possibly teach. Athletics taught me about handling success and dealing with disappointment. Athletics taught me about teamwork and the importance of goal setting. Athletics taught me to get up, even when I didn't want to.

The thing about being a winner is not always about how many times you have won. Nobody wins all the time. It's how many times you have gotten back up after being kicked in the face. That is the true measure of an individual. Lou Holtz once said, "When you suffer a disappointment, it means you did something wrong and need to go back and correct it or change it. So, when you suffer a disappointment, you can make three choices: you can become frustrated, intimidated, or motivated." What separates the successful from the unsuccessful is the ability to persevere.

I loved all sports, but I found my true love in fifth grade. On a hot and humid summer day on August 13, I took the initial step in my football journey. I was excited to start practicing, but also a little nervous. I would be playing with kids who already had a year's experience. My first interaction with my coach was when he instructed me on how to get down in a three-point stance.

I questioned his method, and I said, "But, I thought…."

He quickly cut me off and said, "Don't think, you're not equipped."

Welcome to football! That day was the first time I ever wore a helmet. Wearing that helmet in the heat felt hotter than I imagined the seven rings of hell felt and it only got hotter once we put the pads on. Somewhere in between wishing I were sitting in an air-conditioned grocery store with my face pressed against the linoleum and getting yelled at, I developed the fundamentals of football.

My youth league football coaches were truly great teachers. They were very demanding, but because of that, I learned a work ethic. They conducted practices just like high school practices. We practiced every day for two plus hours and conditioned until we felt like throwing up. Often I did. My first year playing I was a nose tackle and fullback. I had some baby fat and needed to be playing the line. (Actually, I was just fat, but referring to it as baby fat made me feel better.) By my second year I moved to corner and running back. I found my niche. I played Troy Cowboys football for four years. My years playing youth football laid a solid foundation from which I could build a house. But I wanted to build a mansion.

THREE

INSPIRATION

"When you stand for nothing, you fall for anything."

~Maya Angelou~

I am Catholic. I love my faith, and it has helped me through many times in my life when it would have been easy to give up on myself. I do not think it is the only religion that can lead to a healthy and happy life, but I do believe you need to have some power or source to turn to when life gives you rough patches. It may be a religion or it may some other source of inspiration. I chose to minor in theology at Notre Dame because I wanted to gain a better understanding of that which is such a powerful motivator for so many people.

There is a story of three men who are taking their cotton to a cotton gin. The first man takes the northern route, which has nice paved roads to travel. The second man takes the most direct road in which he has to traverse over a mountain. The third man takes the southern route, which has many winding roads and dangerous obstacles. All three men arrive at the cotton gin at the same time.

When they get there the man at the cotton gin does not say, "Which road did you take to get here?"

He simply asks, "Brother, how good is your cotton?"

The moral of the story is that it does not matter what road you take in life or what religion you are, as long as you are trying to live a life in harmony with your values.

For all of recorded history, philosophers and theologians have attempted to unveil the mysteries surrounding such questions as:

1. Is there any purpose to human existence?
2. What is life and how has it developed?
3. Does the rational structure of the universe mean it must have resulted from the work of an omnipotent being?

These are pretty heavy questions. Attempting to answer these concretely would take an eternity. Somewhere in our search for the answers we have to rely on faith. Faith, by definition, is belief in that for which there is no proof. But proof can be found on a daily basis if we just look around at the world and all that humans are able to accomplish.

The three things I think are important in successful people are faith, staying positive, and confidence. Faith—God has a plan and will use our talents to help others. Staying positive—good things are going to happen even when life is a struggle; that is, believing it is the hard times that are going to make the good times that much better. And confidence—believing in your abilities even when other people do not. It is not always about aptitude. More often than not, it is about attitude. How you approach each day will determine your future. And only you can control the attitude you choose to embrace each day. That is the amazing gift we all have, but we must claim it.

There is a reason we can do more than just seek food and procreate. That is what separates us from the animals. Nobody has to tell a bird how to fly to warmer climates when it turns cold. There is no weatherman giving them a forecast and Rand McNally is not providing them with maps. Yet, somehow they are able to fly thousands of miles to warmer climates in the anticipation of cold weather. A squirrel does not have to experience his first winter without food to know he has to start saving up nuts for the cold season. Why? Because of instinct. As humans, we have been given a conscience and the ability to set goals and go after them. That is what makes us special. That is what makes us unique. We have been given free will and we have been blessed with more than just instincts. It is the intellect of human beings that differentiates us from the animals. Humans can use their will to follow good behavior. We also have the power to resist the flow of over-indulgence.

That is a daily challenge. As Aristotle said, "I count him braver who overcomes his desires than he who conquers his enemies; for the hardest victory is victory over self."

But, sometimes I wonder if we couldn't learn something from our friends in the animal kingdom. While we certainly have been blessed with the ability to have complex emotions and are capable of creating a myriad of languages and cultures, maybe we are missing something. What if animals had the ability to know they were being cruel or hurtful, had the ability to lie, or could find ways to change reality (alcohol and drugs)? Would they exploit it and take advantage as much as their human counterparts? What if, when we knew we had been cruel or hurtful, we always made it a point to reconcile and apologize or, better yet, not be cruel in the first place? Or what if drugs and alcohol were never abused? Think of how many lives would be changed for the better. Think of how far reaching the results would be if only we did not exploit our gifts and turn them into weaknesses. Indeed, much can be learned from our friends in the animal kingdom.

Faith, to me, is a foundation. If you have a solid foundation, you can overcome any obstacle that might impede your progress. There is a reason they say there are no atheists in a foxhole. I have never seen the aftermath of a hurricane. But I can imagine it uproots trees, displaces cars, and mangles homes. After a hurricane hits, what is left of once beautiful homes is not the brick, wood, or support beams. All that remains of a once proud home is the foundation. And such is life. If you have a solid foundation on which you have built your values and you have a positive outlook, there is nothing that can break you. My parents provided me with that strong foundation. I was fortunate to have two loving parents, but there is always someone worthy of respect, whether it be a teacher, a friend, or some other mentor that can be used as a role model for life.

My mom has been a teacher for eighteen years. To help put me through Notre Dame, she took a job teaching second grade in the Detroit public schools. She loves to teach and that is why she is plying her trade in one of the neediest school districts in the country. Many of the Detroit public schools are understaffed, lacking supplies, and functioning in old broken buildings. Her school is no exception. Many times she has come home in tears, exhausted with frustration at the lack of equality of opportunity her students have. Most are from single parent homes and several have parents who are in prison. Her labor of love and sacrifice to help pay for my college education is something for which I could never adequately thank her. I have been accused of being a momma's boy. That's okay with me, because she instilled in me a belief I could do anything I set my mind to. For that, I will be forever grateful.

My dad supported me in every endeavor. Unlike some overbearing fathers, he never tried to live vicariously through me. He allowed me to discover my interests and talents on my own without always pushing and cajoling me in the direction he thought best. He did not try and breed me from the womb to be anything other than what I wanted to be. Because I was trying to live my own dreams, I think it made me push myself that much harder. Although, thinking back, I guess I was slowly, sublimely brainwashed to love Notre Dame. For that, I thank him.

I am inspired by the work ethic and commitment of both my mother and father. Even when times were difficult, they never failed to provide for our family. They taught me obstacles are merely a source of knowledge, and we learn about ourselves more in times of struggle than we do during times of success. They are both my daily source of inspiration.

But, the summer before my freshman year of high school I had inspiration hit me from another source. I was sitting in the waiting room of a doctor's office, thumbing through a magazine. While reading an article about college athletics, I came across an interesting quote I tore out of the magazine and stuck in my wallet. I had a typical long wait in the doctor's office that day, and motivation seemed to be coming at me from all directions. I picked up another magazine and read a quote by Abraham Lincoln that I also tore out and placed in my wallet. Both of these quotes provided motivation for me when I needed inspiration or I was having a hard time physically or mentally. Though I carried the quotes with me every day, I had all but forgotten they were in my wallet, until one day in the fall—nine years later.

FOUR

HIGH SCHOOL

"Be who you are and say what you feel, because those who mind don't matter and those who matter don't mind."

~Dr. Seuss~

High school is a time when you are defined by many aesthetic things. A zit seems life threatening, standing up for what you believe in could cost you "cool points," and you must have the right brand name on your jeans. I cannot say I did not buy into many of these established stereotypes. But I always had a strong sense of who I was and where I wanted to go. I think you have to have long-range goals to keep you from being frustrated by short-range disappointments. I was blessed to have a group of friends who were able to balance the pressures of high school while still maintaining their sense of self. Athletics made the transition into high school that much easier for me.

There are many events going on in the life of a fifteen-year-old entering high school. You are entering into a new environment where peer pressure begins to intensify and temptations begin to slowly pull on your conscience. Whether it is the pressure of alcohol, drugs, or sex, there is certainly no shortage of opportunity to head down the wrong path. It is important to align yourself with a group of friends who share similar interests. There are always going to be people who try and bring you down. Rarely is it ever a conscience choice to hang out with people whose values do not coincide with your own; it is just a situation in which you find yourself. That is why you must make a concerted effort *not* to allow yourself to head down a questionable path with questionable people. Thinking for yourself and having a clear idea of where you want to be in ten years is not an easy thing to do—especially for a teenager. You must constantly fight human nature and laziness. Ralph Waldo Emerson said, "Two roads diverged in the wood. And I, I chose the one less traveled by, and that has made all the difference." We could all do well, to heed his advice. We can either be *influenced* by our environment or *influence* our environment. I think the challenge is to do the latter.

I was fortunate to find solace in sports throughout my four years at Athens High School in Troy, Michigan. I formed and enriched many lasting friendships through my participation in athletics. I truly believe sports prevented me from making bad decisions in other areas of high school life. That is why I believe the value of athletics is so much more than wins and losses. Athletics teach valuable life lessons and provide after-school activities that do not revolve around alcohol or drugs. Many high school kids find sports to be a natural high. I was no exception.

During my freshman and sophomore years at Athens High School, I played football, basketball, and baseball. Football and basketball were my two best sports. I played baseball mostly to give me something to do in the springtime. My sophomore year of football, I had visions of grandeur in my head. In our first game we won 36-30. My friend scored the first touchdown, and with the help of my lineman, I scored the next thirty points (four touchdowns and three two-point conversions). I had over 250 yards rushing, and it was a good way to start the season from an individual and team standpoint. During the next seven games I scored sixteen touchdowns and gained over 1,600 yards rushing. I was in my heyday. I carried the ball around twenty-five times a game, and I loved every minute of it. I had similar success in basketball my first two years. I was awarded MVP honors as a freshman, and my sophomore year I was in the top two in almost every statistical category. I only mention these things to preface what happened my junior year.

After my sophomore football season, I expected my junior year to be more of the same. My friend, whom I grew up with, Nathan Wize, moved to Arizona after middle school because his parents felt he had a better chance at a college scholarship if he played his high school football in Arizona. They had a good relationship with one of the coaches in Arizona, and they knew he would watch Nathan closely and look out for his best interests. However, before my junior year, he moved back to Michigan. Nathan and I had always been very competitive with each other. He was one of my best friends. He had played varsity as a sophomore in Arizona and now was going to be my teammate. He was a tailback and so was I. There was only one tailback in our offense, so the coaches decided to move Nathan to fullback so he and I could both be on the field at the same time. He was a little bigger than I was, so it seemed like the logical choice. In our first game we played Oak Park and we won 31-6. Nathan had 126 yards rushing on eleven carries and two touchdowns. I had 131 yards rushing on sixteen carries and two touchdowns. We were off to a good start.

But after our second game, Nathan decided to move back to Arizona. He had the flexibility to move to Arizona because his coach there had taken legal guardianship of him so he would be eligible to play football in Arizona. Since our high school had never produced a Division I scholarship football player, I think he and his parents saw the writing on the wall in terms of not getting much exposure to potential college recruiters at our high school. He went on to become the all-time single season rushing leader in Arizona high school football history. He finished his senior year with 3,101 yards rushing and fifty-one touchdowns. His record-breaking season earned him a full-ride scholarship to the University of Cincinnati.

We finished my junior year 6-3 after starting 5-0 and did not qualify for the state playoffs. I finished the season with eight hundred yards rushing and averaged 7.2 yards per carry. A good average per carry, but not the stats that get the attention of college recruiters. I was also named one of the top five underclassman in the county by the *Oakland Press*. The *Oakland Press* is a paper serving the Oakland County, Michigan, area. There are seventy-four high schools in the Oakland County school district, so to be selected as one of the top five underclassmen football players by the paper was an honor. Also selected was another future Notre Dame football player, Javin Hunter, a future Indiana basketball player, Dane Fife, and a future Ohio State football player, Ricky Bryant.

After football ended, I turned my attention to basketball. After being MVP as a freshman on a 19-1 team and having similar success my sophomore year, I viewed the tryouts as a technicality. The tryout process consisted mostly of conditioning drills, jump roping, and running. We did not touch a basketball until the last couple days of tryouts. I had done well in all of the conditioning drills, and I was confident I had proven myself as much as the tryouts allowed. On the last day of tryouts I was called into the coach's office to hear what I viewed as the inevitable. When the coach informed me I did not make the team, I was momentarily speechless.

All I could mutter before I left his office was, "I think you underestimate me."

I walked out into the hallway away from earshot and laid down and cried harder than I ever had in my life. I thought I was having a bad dream. It was the single most disappointing thing that had ever happened to me up to that point. I truly felt like someone close to me had died. I had been playing basketball for a long time and now I did not know what to do with myself. I had something taken from me that was near and dear to my heart that day. For the next month I could hardly eat, was sleeping a lot, and just generally feeling sorry for myself.

After I came out of my funk, I decided to turn the negative into a positive. I decided to focus all of my energy into preparing myself for the upcoming football season. It was then that I decided not to play baseball either. I wanted to do everything I could to reach my goal of getting a scholarship to Notre Dame. The odds certainly weren't in my favor. I had read a pamphlet from the NCAA discussing the probability of achieving a Division I football scholarship. It read:

Example: NCAA Football

    107 Division I Schools

x   85 Scholarships allowed per school

    9,095 total scholarships, nationally

−   6,955 approximate number of returning players nationally

    2,140 available scholarships for approximately 1 million high school senior football players

After doing some simple division, that placed my odds firmly at .214 percent.

I began running through the halls of my school at night while the basketball team was practicing. I made great strides in my strength training during that time. All I did was run and lift weights. Many nights after seeing a movie with my friends or girlfriend, I went to my high school track to do a sprint workout and run the bleachers. Push-ups and sit-ups became a prerequisite before going to bed at night or I'd feel guilty and get out of bed and do them. I took the approach of "Nobody in the country works harder than me (N.I.T.C.W.H.T.M.)." If I didn't reach my goals, I did not want it to be because of lack of effort. I would write N.I.T.C.W.H.T.M on folders, under the brim of my hats, or any other place where it would serve as a constant reminder of what I needed to strive for in order to reach my goals.

The next season I began living a dream because I was elected captain of the football team and I was dating the homecoming queen, Mandi Lonero. Her becoming homecoming queen came as no surprise to me because she had truly been a queen in my eyes for the nearly two years we had been dating. She won because of her beauty, yes, but also because she was a genuine person whom other people respected.

My senior year, I achieved almost the exact same statistics as the previous season with 832 yards rushing. I finished my Troy Athens High School football career with 1,631 yards rushing and over 2,000 yards rushing and receiving. However, mine was only a decent high school career and not the stuff that makes college coaches drool. To compound my problem, I was 5' 6" and only weighed 165 pounds. Some Division II and III schools recruited me, but I had my heart set on playing Division I. I sent fifteen highlight tapes to different Division I schools before my senior season. I was invited to walk-on at a couple of them but received no scholarship offers. I received a postcard from Notre Dame saying they had received my tape. But I never heard anything else. I figured they did not want me. *Did they even see my tape?* It became apparent a scholarship offer for me was not going to be forthcoming. It looked like I was going to have to go to plan B.

FIVE

PLAN B

"Just out of curiosity, do we have a plan B?"

~Nathan Lane as Preed in Titan A.E.~

ince attending Notre Dame on a football scholarship was no longer an option, I developed a plan B. The first stage of this plan involved getting accepted to Notre Dame, because without an acceptance letter it would not have mattered how badly I wanted to play football. The second stage of the plan involved getting the attention of the football coaches so they would invite me to be part of the team as a non-scholarship player.

There are two ways to become a part of a Division I college football team: to earn a scholarship out of high school, or to become a walk-on. Walking on to a Division I football team usually occurs in one of two ways. There are "preferred walk-ons" who don't have to go through a tryout process because they have already been evaluated by the coaches on film or through word of mouth endorsements based on a solid high school career. And then there are walk-ons who try out for the team during a spring semester tryout process. In either scenario, the goals of every football player are the same: to contribute and help your team win.

I applied to Notre Dame and a few other schools. I applied to several great schools, but I knew deep down if I didn't get accepted to Notre Dame, there would be a void in my heart. I know another university could have provided a great education and a great experience, but, for me, there was really only one place I ever wanted to go. I essentially put all of my time and energy into the Notre Dame application. I spent hours pouring over my admission essays to Notre Dame, even enlisting the help of my parish priest to generate ideas for my papers. Two mandatory essays are required by the admission's committee, and a third essay about why a prospective student wants to spend four years of his or her life at Notre Dame, is optional. I held nothing back in this optional essay, knowing the essay was my opportunity to express in words what attending Notre Dame would mean to me.

I sent out all of my college applications on the same say, and began the waiting game. I knew the soon-to-be received Notre Dame rejection or acceptance letter was either going to completely devastate me, or provide a life changing opportunity. Admission committees can be fickle sometimes, so I really did not know if the letter arriving at my house would be a thin one or a thick one. After checking the mail daily, the letter finally came. It was thick. The only person home to celebrate with was my dog, Bailey. He looked at me like I was crazy. But, proving dogs are indeed a man's best friend, he jumped around and yelped right along with me. It looked like half of my dream was within my reach. When my parents got home, my smile conveyed the news. Even though today I know my parents wondered then how we would pay for it, at the time, they never let me think they wouldn't find a way to make it happen.

The same day I found out I was accepted, I called the football recruiting coordinator at Notre Dame, Bob Chmiel. Coach Chmiel had also been given the responsibility of overseeing the walk-on program from Coach Holtz. I told Coach Chmiel I had been accepted to the school, and I was interested in walking-on. I wanted to be a part of the team from day one and not have to miss a whole season of learning by having to wait until the spring tryout process. I wanted to start when all the other freshman football players started so I could measure myself against my peers.

I'm sure Coach Chmiel received several calls from high school dreamers every day. He encouraged me and gave me the same cookie cutter answers I imagine everyone received.

He said, "When you come to campus, work hard your freshman year and come try out in the spring."

Try out in the spring! That would put me a whole half semester behind where I wanted to be. Over the next week I debated on what my next course of action would be. I decided to put all of my energy into one more highlight tape. I needed to get noticed. I sat down for hours with all of my game film and two VCRs and put together a tape of my best plays. Before I sent the tape, I included in it newspaper clippings from the season and a letter of recommendation from my high school head coach, John Walker. I also told a bold-faced lie. I wrote down my height and weight as 5' 9", 175 pounds. Three days after I sent the tape I received a phone call.

When the phone rang I was half a sleep and expecting a call from a friend.

Uncharacteristically, I answered the phone, "Yeah?"

At the other end of the line were words I had been waiting to hear for most of my life. "Hi, Timmy. This is Bob Chmiel, University of Notre Dame football," he stated in his native Chicagoan way.

I bolted right out of my sleep-induced coma and stood up. I managed to mutter the words, "Hi, coach, how you doing?"

He told me he had received my tape and the coaches wanted me to walk-on. And so I said, "You want me to come and try out?"

And he said, "No, we want you to come here, get your physical, and join the team."

We talked a little bit more, but I don't remember any words discussed. I hung up the phone and questioned whether or not I heard him right. *Did he just say I was on the team?* I pinched myself. I knew I wasn't dreaming. This time my dog was not the only one home to help me celebrate. My parents were also home to hear the news. I will never forget the opportunity Coach Chmiel presented to me, and for that, I will always be indebted to him. My life as a walk-on would begin in the fall of 1998, and at the time I had no idea where the journey would take me.

NCAA rules state a maximum of one hundred and five football players may be invited to pre-season camp. Pre-season camp usually starts the first week of August and involves grueling twice-a-day practices. With eighty-five players on full scholarship, that only leaves twenty roster spots for walk-ons to fill. I was hoping to be invited to camp because if I was not, the rules stated I would have to wait until school started to begin practicing with the team. Waiting would be a disadvantage for two reasons. One, I would be two weeks behind my teammates in terms of learning. Two, I would be missing out on the camaraderie the blood, sweat, and tears the two-a-day practices provide. A week before fall camp was to start, I learned I would not be invited to camp because they already reached the limit of one hundred and five players. I suspect the real reason was maybe they found out I was really 5' 6" and not the 5' 9" I claimed to be on my recruiting profile. But I was assured a spot would be waiting for me when school started. I felt disappointed, but not discouraged. I was going to be on the team and that is all that mattered to me at the time.

The first day of school I went to the football office to talk to Coach Chmiel about when I could start practice. At the time he was my savior because he was the only coach who knew my name. Coach Chmiel informed me they would be taking three additional freshman walk-ons onto the team: John Crowther, a snapper; Matt Sarb, a safety; and me, a tailback. I later found out there were three other walk-ons who had been invited to the one-hundred-and-five player party who had already been practicing for two weeks: Adam Tibble, a kicker; and two defensive backs, Patrick Reynolds and Dewayne Francis. There were a total of six freshman walk-ons who joined the team in the fall of 1998.

Matt Sarb and I happened to be in the same dorm, Stanford Hall. I introduced myself to him and informed him I was going to be on the team too. We had a common bond in that we both had always dreamed of playing football at Notre Dame. We hit it off right away, probably because we saw a little bit of each other in the other person. Matt's family also had a long history with the university. His great grandparents lived next door to legendary coach Knute Rockne, and when Rockne converted to Catholicism, they were his confirmation sponsors. Matt's father, Pat Sarb, also had been a football player at Notre Dame. The more I talked to Matt, the more I realized how similar our backgrounds were. If I had a long lost twin brother, it would have been Matt. We quickly united forces to try and start practicing as quickly as possible, and we each probably called the football office five times a day.

Our starting date with the Notre Dame football team kept getting pushed back for one reason or another. We were given thorough physicals, followed by speed and strength testing. We had to run the forty-yard dash twice and get tested in how many times we could bench press 225 pounds.

In my first forty-yard dash, the strength coach lined up at the goal line, and I lined up on the forty-yard line. The strength coach started the stopwatch on my movement. When I crossed the goal line I was a little disappointed in my time. It was a fast time, but it wasn't Division I tailback fast. *I can't blow this.* We were already told we were on the team, but we both knew there was nothing to prevent the coaches from changing their minds. After Sarb ran his forty, he too, was a little disappointed in his time. As we jogged back to the forty-yard line I think we both thought the same thing at the same time. The strength coach was down at the other end of the field and could not see where we lined up. So we both turned a forty-yard dash into a thirty-eight-and-a-half-yard dash on our second runs. As I crossed the goal line two-tenths of a second faster than on my previous run, I felt a lot more confident I was still going to be on the team. Sarb's time was also two-tenths of a second better on his second run.

"See, you two just needed to get warmed up," the strength coach offered.

Wait 'til you see my thirty-seven-yard dash time. I justified our Machiavellian abbreviated forty-yard dash the same way I justified lying about my height and weight on my recruiting profile. All I needed was the door to Notre Dame football to be opened just enough so I could stick my foot inside—then I would spend the rest of my football career trying to prove to the people who opened it for me they had made the right decision. Following the forty-yard dash, Matt and I bench pressed 225 pounds as many times as possible. I managed to press the weight seven times, which is not very good. So I guess I was slow *and* weak.

The promise of starting practice the first day of school did not come to fruition. Nor did it in the second week. Matt and I had been told we were likely going to be starting our college careers on August 7, when the whole team reported for fall camp. That didn't happen. Then we were told we were going to start the first week of school. That didn't happen because we had to get our physicals and get tested. Then the line of the day became we were going to start after the Michigan game, which was the first game of the season. But, rather than celebrating on the field after defeating the defending co-national champions, Matt and I sat watching from the stands. It was the only home game in my five years at Notre Dame I watched from the stands, and I hated every minute of it. I felt like the little kid in the candy store who was only allowed to look at the exquisite candies through the glass. I was so close, but yet so far away.

Finally, it was decided Matt and I would start after the Michigan State game because we had a bye week after that game to prepare for our next opponent. During the time of uncertainty about when we would be starting Matt and I began getting restless. We collectively must have made over one hundred calls to the football office asking the seemingly unanswerable question of "When can we start?" We had already gotten our physicals, had already been tested, and now we just needed to get fitted for our uniforms.

With anticipation equal only to a little child waiting for Christmas morning, the day finally arrived to get our uniforms. We went into the locker room and then were led to the equipment room, which is essentially a storage space built underneath the stadium steps. There were rows of uniforms, stacks of tennis shoes, and every conceivable football amenity ever made—except for a pair of size 8 1/2 cleats. Apparently they never had a need for that size in the football program before I needed them. So I was issued a pair of size 9s that was fished out of a bin with cobwebs on it. I would have to make do with the 9s until they could special order the right size. *No problem, I'll just wear two pairs of socks.*

After getting fitted with shoulder pads, kneepads, thigh pads, and every other piece of equipment we needed to get started, Matt and I were issued our jersey numbers. I was issued #35, and Matt was issued #45. I was just happy to have a number. In fact, I didn't know it at the time, but #35 would also serve as my name for the next few weeks. It was easier for the coaches to remember the number staring back at them at practice than it was for them to remember a name. So "Hey, Thirty-five," became my name while I tried to make a positive impression. Matt's #45 also happened to be the same number Rudy wore. My walk-on teammates and I loved calling him Rudy. He hated it. So we did what any good friends would do—we did it more.

After being given our pads and assigned jersey numbers, we had only one piece of equipment left to receive. The equipment manager wheeled out the gold helmets and we began the process of trying them on. I couldn't believe it! I was going to wear the same hallowed helmet I had seen the student managers painting on my first ever visit to the stadium with my dad. The helmets looked different than the ones I saw on TV every Saturday because none of them had facemasks on them and they had yet to be painted. When our equipment manager, Chris Matlock, placed the different sizes on my head, I found one that fit perfectly. I felt as if I had arrived. Putting that helmet on for the first time is a feeling I'll never forget. Also, a feeling I tried to remember in the years that followed when human nature set in and I started to get frustrated.

Matt and I now had our uniforms, so the final piece of the puzzle was being assigned a locker. Matt and I were assigned lockers in the visitors' locker room. Such is the life of a freshman walk-on because all of the lockers in the storied locker room were already taken. I would later find out among the walk-ons having to get dressed in the visitors' locker room was referred to as the "walk of shame." It was so named because after completing classes for the day, all the football players walked through the stadium gate and into the locker room to get ready for practice—except the chosen few who had to walk into the locker room to pick up their clean laundry for the day's practice, then leave the locker room and walk about fifty feet to get dressed and ready for practice in the visitors' locker room. This fifty-foot walk was known as the walk of shame, because you felt like an unwanted member of the team exiled to another part of the stadium to get dressed, out of sight and out of mind.

When the equipment manager led us into the visitors' locker room, we had our choice of fifty lockers because only four of the lockers had equipment in them. We would later learn four other walk-ons, in addition to Matt and me, enjoyed the benefit of having a locker in the visitors' locker room. Something must have been in the water on that side of the stadium though, because out of six of us who got dressed in the visitors' locker room that year, today, counted among those six, are four doctors, one lawyer, and me. They make me feel like a failure. Once we got past the feeling of isolation, getting dressed in the visitors' locker room actually had its advantages. We could take up about three lockers with our things, and we had a lot more space than our counterparts in the main locker room. After the equipment manager left Matt and me alone in the locker room, we staked out our spaces and placed our equipment inside the lockers. We were now ready to begin our football careers.

No one ever told Matt or me when we could start practice. But we had our physicals, uniforms, lockers, and we knew what time practice started. So in our minds, we had everything we needed to begin practicing. Besides, we were tired of waiting. On the Monday following our game against Michigan State, we decided we were just going to get dressed and head out to practice. My first practice as a college football player was in full pads. There was no grace period because the season was already in full swing. We did not really have any idea what was going on once we got out there because everyone was just running around.

We found a spot in the back of the calisthenics' line and then we saw the head manager got a phone call and said, "Tim O'Neill? Matt Sarb?"

He hangs up the phone, finds out who we are, and says, "You two guys have to go back to the football office and fill out paperwork."

We trudged back to the football office in our full football regalia and were greeted by an angry recruiting coordinator. Coach Chmiel started yelling at us that we could have gotten everyone in trouble because we did not fill out the proper paperwork, and he told us we couldn't practice until the next day. So we went back into the locker room with our pads on and just started hitting each other. We had so much energy and just could not wait any longer to get out on the field. We stayed in the locker room and got down in three-point stances and just knocked each other until we were dripping with sweat. The next day would be the official beginning of my life as a Notre Dame football player.

SIX

PRACTICE AND POLICE CHASES

"And everywhere I went from that day on, I was running."

~Tom Hanks as Forrest Gump~

efore every practice, every position works in separate groups where the players do their stretching and individual drills. On my first official day of practice I introduced myself to the running back coach, Desmond Robinson, and he introduced me to my new teammates, including two other walk-ons, Jeremy Juarez and Jascint Vukelich, both fullbacks. I was a little bit intimidated on that first day. Here I was, a 5' 6", 165-pound freshman along with the likes of future NFL players Autry Denson, Jamie Spencer, and Joey Goodspeed, not to mention my fellow classmates, high school all-Americans, Tommy Lopienski and Mike McNair. These were some big dudes. I thought to myself, if one of these guys starts something I'm either going to have to kick them in the stomach and run or I'm going to have to dive at their ankles and try and bite them. But, luckily, since day one they accepted me into their family.

I soon became familiar with the structure of practices. After warming up with our individual position for fifteen minutes, the entire team lined up together and did another set of stretching and calisthenics. Next came twenty-four periods of practice. Each period was between five and fifteen minutes long, depending on the mood of the head coach. The ending of every period was accompanied by an air horn signaling it was time to switch drills. The content of the periods ranged from one-on-one blocking drills to team offense versus team defense scrimmages.

My first opportunity to carry the ball came against our first team defense. I was running tailback on our scout team offense, and I lined up in the huddle while our graduate assistant coach, Jay Savelle, held up a card, which showed how the play was to be run. The card looked like this:

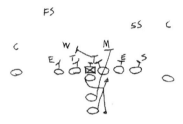

This basically meant the quarterback was going to reverse pivot and hand me the ball on an isolation play. The fullback was isolated against the linebacker, and I had it in my mind I was just going to follow my fullback. This seemed like the best thing to do on my first ever college football carry, since my fullback was Jeremy Juarez, a 5' 11", 251-pound human wrecking ball.

I lined up in the backfield, surveyed the defense, and waited for the quarterback to go through his cadence. The quarterback was Zak Kustok, who, at the end of the season, would transfer to Northwestern and go on to have a great career with the Wildcats.

"Here goes nothing," I whispered to myself as Kustok started his cadence.

"Blue 81, Blue 81, Set, Hit!" he shouted.

With that, I took one drop-step and followed my fullback through the hole. As I passed through the line of scrimmage, I saw an opening to the left side behind the center, and I instinctively cut it back. Our linebacker over pursued, and I was able to run by him into the secondary. I sprinted untouched until I couldn't run anymore because I had run into another defensive drill on the opposite side of the field. I was feeling pretty good about myself as I jogged back to the huddle, and thought I might even get a compliment from one of the defensive coaches for taking it to the house against his starting defense.

But when I got back to within earshot, the linebackers' coach started screaming at me, "Son, what in the Sam Hell are you doing?"

I just stood there because I figured he was going to tell me what I had done wrong. When he didn't elaborate, I finally said, "I was just…."

He quickly cut me off, "You were just…what? What did the card say to do? Did the card say to cut that play back?"

"No, sir," I replied.

"No, sir, is right. Now huddle back up and run the damn play again, you slap! And run it right this time!"

It turned out "Slap," in addition to "Hey, Thirty-five," would serve as my name until the coaches could remember who I was. But this actually wasn't too bad compared to the name my friend and teammate Eddie O'Connell was given.

His coach asked him one day, "What's your name, son? Pat?"

"Eddie, sir," he responded.

"Well, your damn name should be Pat."

And with that he proceeded to keep calling him Pat until he was deemed worthy of going by the name his parents gave him.

After being reprimanded on my first ever carry, I decided I was going to do exactly what the card said when we ran the play again. I lined up in the backfield again and surveyed the defense. This time they appeared a little more ready than on the previous play. I waited for the cadence, took the handoff, and followed the fullback through the hole. I ran off the right side of the line, just as the card told me to do. I got a great block from Juarez on the play-side linebacker, but the backside linebacker, whom I had run by on the previous play, blasted me from the side with a vengeance. My left ear was ringing as my body was thrown to the ground. As soon as I hit the ground I hopped right back to my feet because I didn't want to appear weak on my first day of practice as the new guy on the team. I checked to make sure everything was still working as I ran back to the huddle with my eardrum still ringing from the collision.

I heard the linebackers' coach say, "That's better, Thirty-five," as I ran back to the huddle.

That's better? Better for whom? Maybe for the guy who just hit me, but it certainly wasn't better for me. I looked over at our linebackers' coach and he smiled back at me. I think he knew what I must have been thinking. So after my first two carries, I promised myself every time I carried the ball I was going to carry the ball as if I were in a real game. If that meant following a hole not written on a card, so be it. I viewed my roles as a walk-on as helping the defense get better and proving to the coaches I was good enough to play so I wouldn't be on the scout team the rest of my career. I didn't feel either of those roles would be fulfilled if I didn't allow myself to just go out and play football as I always had since I was in fourth grade. If the linebackers' coach wouldn't have yelled at me, it would have taken me longer to figure out how things worked.

I'm glad I learned that lesson on day one, rather than later in my career. There would be plenty more times I would get my bell rung during my next five years, but it would never happen again because of me acting as a sacrificial lamb being lead into the slaughter by failing to run the ball using my instincts.

After my first practice, Coach Chmiel introduced me to our head coach, Bob Davie. That was my first interaction with the man who would see more of me than my own parents during the next four years. With all of the people he met, Coach Davie probably forgot my name after that first encounter. I would make sure I did something for him to remember it.

The next few months of my life revolved around going to class and then going to football practice every night for four hours. I quickly became acclimated to the college game because I played the scout team tailback from day one of practice. The coaches put me in the backfield, and I ran the opponent's plays against our first string defense. It was unbelievably exciting for me.

People often ask me "How was college football different from high school?"

The difference is the size of the players and the speed of the game. Both of which contribute to a lot harder hitting. But in my opinion that was the only real difference. To me, football is football. I felt I had been coached very well throughout my high school career, so I did not feel overwhelmed or at a disadvantage at all. The players were all very talented, but I did not feel like they were heads and tails above me in terms of ability. Perhaps that was because of my brothers always telling me to not underestimate myself and my abilities, but I did not see any reason why, with hard work, I did not have a chance to contribute on the field in the next couple years.

I tried to get involved in as many drills as I could. I got kicked out of many drills and had a scholarship player put in front of me. That was just how football practice was for a walk-on. You had to be relentless and have a thick skin. If I did not stay positive and keep trying to get involved, it would have been very easy to get discouraged. The highlight of my week was the days in practice when we would go full pads. This meant I'd get to carry the ball a lot and go against our first team defense. I always looked forward to the days in full pads because it meant I'd have an opportunity to get noticed.

One of our assistant coaches my freshman year was a man named Charlie Strong. He, as of this writing, is the defensive coordinator at the University of Florida and is an up-and-coming future head coach. He was one of the coaches I admired most because he always took the time to get to know the player's name and find out a little bit about him. It is no coincidence he has risen through the ranks.

I remember one of the first days of practice I was in the locker room picking up my clean laundry for the day (since I had to carry it back to the visitors' locker room to get dressed). Coach Strong was in the locker room, and he asked me the typical getting-to-know-you type questions: my name, where I was from, what position I played, etc. I think he was a little surprised by my size and wanted to know a little bit more about me. I told him all of my information and told him I was a tailback. He asked me how many yards I had in high school, and I told him I had over 2,000. That was pretty much the end of the conversation.

Over the next couple weeks of practice, every time Coach Strong saw me in the stretch lines he said to no one in particular, "That's Tiny Tim. The all-time leading rusher in the state of Michigan." I knew I wasn't the all-time leading rusher in the state of Michigan. He knew too. But he just said it to build my confidence. One day before practice, I was standing in our stretch line and Coach Davie was doing his daily walk around the players, occasionally stopping to talk to one of us. On this particular day he came by and talked to me.

He said, "Tiny Tim, were you the all-time leading rusher in the state of Michigan?"

And I said, "No, coach, I was close though."

Coach Strong made people pay attention to me. It wasn't much, but it was enough to have the head coach remember my name.

I did not dress for a game until the last game of my freshman year. By the time I suited up, I had contributed two-and-a-half months of blood, sweat, and tears to the football program. We were playing LSU and the feeling I got when I ran out of the tunnel in front of eighty thousand screaming fans cannot be put into words. That was the first moment it really hit me—I was playing football for Notre Dame. I'll never forget that day as long as I live.

The game was a back-and-forth seesaw battle ending in a Notre Dame victory to bring our record to 9-1. It was also an infamous game because our starting quarterback, Jarious Jackson, was injured on the last play of the game while taking an intentional safety. Without our starting quarterback we lost our last game of the year to USC and ended our chances of playing in a Bowl Championship Series (BCS) game.

After the regular season finished, we had a few days off to study and complete our final exams before we began practicing for the Gator Bowl. During practices the campus was deserted because the entire student body, save the football team, went home for Christmas vacation. Our schedule was very regimented—practice, meetings, and workouts occupied most of our day. But in the evenings, we had a little more free time than usual because we had no schoolwork to keep us occupied since classes weren't in session.

After one of the bowl-week practices, Coach Davie called up the team and offered this advice, "It's just like when we started fall camp; there's no one else on this campus but us. Remember why we're here and don't do anything tonight that will jeopardize the reputation of this football team."

It was later in the evening when Matt Sarb and I were sitting in our vacated dorm pondering the prospect of another boring night in South Bend, Indiana. We bounced around a few ideas to entertain ourselves before settling on a nighttime adventure that would take us on an exploration of two buildings that were under construction on campus.

There was a new bookstore being built, and the main building with the famous golden dome was undergoing a renovation. The idea behind our clandestine journey was to sneak into the buildings under the veil of darkness so we could take some pictures for posterity's sake.

The first building we decided to infiltrate was the bookstore. We had little trouble gaining access since the doors had not yet been fitted with doorknobs—we just pushed our way inside. While making our way around the first floor, we stepped over two-by-fours and stray nails as the smell of sawdust wafted through the air. Our undercover operation led us to what appeared to be the boiler room where we stumbled upon a metal staircase leading to a trap door in the ceiling. Upon scaling the stairs we pushed through the trap door, expecting it to be locked. It wasn't. The door led to the roof of the building, and Matt and I both climbed on top. From the apex of the bookstore we could see the entire campus spread out under the moonlight. It was one of the prettiest views of the campus I had ever seen. And, while I liked Matt, I would have rather had that pretty girl I had seen in the dining hall with me to share the view.

With our confidence high after getting some great photo opportunities from the roof of the bookstore, we sojourned across campus to tackle our next obstacle—scaling the chain link fence surrounding the Main Building. The Golden Dome caught the light of the moon as Matt and I slowly approached the steps of the main entrance. Our goal was once again simple—find a way to get inside, explore the progress that was being made in the renovation process, take a couple of pictures, and get out. We never had a chance to institute our plan because the shadowy figure of a woman holding a flashlight emerged from the entranceway to the building. Still one hundred yards away, we halted in our tracks, and I could just make out a silver badge on the woman's chest.

Before we could explain ourselves, the officer aimed her flashlight on us and said, "You two better just stop because there's already backup on the way."

There's already backup on the way? My mind raced with reckless abandon about what could possibly have warranted a call for backup. My immediate thought was someone must have vandalized the inside of the Main Building, and Matt and I were going to get blamed for it. Coach Davie's words began to play in a broken record in my mind, "Don't do anything tonight that will jeopardize the reputation of this football team." The words taunted me as I decided on what my next course of action would be. I could only imagine my future football career if the head coach received a phone call at 10:00 at night regarding two of his players trying to break into the Golden Dome. But after all, we hadn't done anything wrong. We would simply explain to the nice officer we only scaled the fence because we wanted to have a look around and take a few innocent pictures. She would be very cordial, and might even take the pictures for us so we wouldn't have to set up the automatic timer. But there still was the risk the officer wouldn't believe a word we said. So we did what anyone else in our situation would do. We ran.

Sarb had no choice but to follow me because I turned and started to run first. We jumped halfway up the fence and pulled ourselves over the top as the beam of the flashlight danced behind us. As soon as we hit the ground a police car pulled within a few feet of where we landed. I pushed off the hood of the car as we continued an all-out sprint away from the flashing lights. If I stopped running now, I would definitely appear guilty. A second police car pulled up closely behind the first as Sarb and I put twenty yards of distance between our pursuers and us.

As we continued to run, a megaphone pierced the still night, "STOP! YOU WILL NOT GET AWAY! STOP!"

Ironically, these words only inspired me to run faster. We managed to get far enough away that the corner of a building momentarily blocked us from view. We decided it was our best chance to try and make it into the safety of our dorm. Sarb fumbled with his keys before finding the right one to unlock the door and we quickly stepped inside and shut the door behind us. Sarb's room was on the first floor and mine was on the third, so we agreed to part ways and decided the next morning we would not leave together at the same time. I silently crept into my room, certain not to turn any lights on that would draw attention to my whereabouts. The entire night a police car continued to circle the parking lot outside my window, lurking like a hungry shark. But the next morning they were gone. Luckily, the identities of the two perpetrators that night were never revealed, and Sarb and I managed to escape a potentially bad situation.

We went on to lose in the Gator Bowl game, but by all accounts we had a solid year. Looking back on the season, I had no regrets about my first year on the team. I had learned to crawl and was looking forward to walking. But in the coming months I would not be doing much walking.

SEVEN

CARLO'S PRISON

"That which does not kill you makes you stronger."

~Quote in Notre Dame weight room~

I remember my first workout with Carlo. It was an exact reincarnation of my vision of hell. It set the stage for all of my other workouts at Notre Dame, and was the reason I knew the off-season was going to be very physically demanding. Matt Sarb and I had become fast friends, and we were about to share in each other's misery. Looking back, I think it was a weeding out process to see if I would run back home to mommy when things got tough. And, believe me, I felt like running home to mommy—I just never admitted that to anyone.

The massacre began in the Joyce Center weight room under the sinister glare of an assistant strength coach named Carlo. The Joyce Center weight room is not where the football players usually work out. But Matt and I were exiled there, I think, in part, to see how badly we wanted to play football for Notre Dame. The football team usually works out in the Loftus Center, but when I started I was not allowed to work out with the rest of the team. For me, I looked at it as having to pay my dues. I wasn't recruited to play at Notre Dame; I had recruited them. They had given me an opportunity to live my dream, and even if that meant they were first going to try and kill me, I was grateful.

I had worked out regularly in high school and considered myself to be in pretty good shape—until that day. It is one thing to be your own strength coach, pushing yourself as far as your mental limits will tolerate; it is another story when Carlo watches your every move. Like a vulcher swarming around a dying carcass, he showed no sympathy for our pain.

Our first exercise was the leg press, which sat unassumingly near the entrance to the weight room. But, most predators are unassuming before seizing their prey. The leg press is a seated apparatus with a platform on which to place your feet. When you sit down in the seat, your knees are bent towards your chest and you place your feet on the platform before extending and contracting your legs. *Seems easy enough.* I volunteered to go first, while Matt did push-ups in front of me. After loading the leg press with more weight than I thought I could do, Carlo made a deal with us. Well, it wasn't so much a deal, as a mandate. Matt would have to do push-ups until I leg pressed the weight Carlo had chosen for me for twenty repetitions.

After willing my legs to press the weight seven times, I could no longer extend them. I was finished, done, caput. I looked at Matt doing push-ups, and I figured it was time for us to switch. But, apparently Carlo was not kidding about having to press the weight twenty times before I could get out of the seat. So, with sheer anger I forced five more repetitions out of my stubborn legs. By this time Matt had done a lot of push-ups, and I wanted him to be able to stop, but my legs simply weren't cooperating despite my best intentions. I had now done twelve reps and my legs were shaking uncontrollably. I had to place my hands on my thighs just to make them stop. I looked up at Carlo with a helpless look, and he looked back and smiled. *Satan, is that you?* He knew I still had eight more to do before I could be released. At this point, every rep was forced using a guttural scream. I inched out one screaming repetition at a time, as I garnered stares from the other lifters in the weight room. I was finally able to complete my twentieth rep after a solid six-minute battle against the machine.

Matt was almost as happy as I was to be done because he could now stop doing push-ups. Now it was my turn to do push-ups while Matt suffered in the chair. I watched him go through what I just did, and I was glad I was done—or so I thought. After Matt finished his set on the leg press, Carlo told me to do a second set. The mere thought of having to get back on the machine made me nauseous.

When I finished my second set on the leg press, I got out of the chair, took two steps, and fell to the ground. My legs were not capable of supporting my own weight. I stood back up triumphantly, before Carlo pointed to the ground and had me do another set of push-ups while Matt completed his second round on the leg press. This battle between man and machine continued throughout various other exercises before Matt had to leave for class. If I had my wits about me I, too, would have said I had a class to go to so I wouldn't have to continue the slow death Carlo had planned for me.

I didn't want Matt to leave. I began to have a flashback of when I was a kindergartner in Mrs. Thompson's class at Hill Elementary School. My mom was dropping me off for my first day of school, and when we walked into the classroom, she was holding me pinned to her hip, with both my little arms slung around her neck. When I saw the other kids sitting cross-legged on the red carpet in front of the chalkboard, I realized I had been tricked. This wasn't going to be fun at all. I wanted my day filled with cartoons and peanut butter and jelly sandwiches (with the crusts cut off, of course), not whatever these dorks sitting on the red carpet had to offer. So when my mom tried to lower me to the carpet to begin my academic career, I clung to her neck with all the strength my five-year-old body could summon.

"Come on, Timmy, school is going to be fun. Let go of Mommy," my mom pleaded.

I pondered silently: *More fun than watching Transformers and He-Man? I don't think so.* While I screamed bloody murder, Mrs. Thompson, bless her heart, tried to help matters by coaxing me out of my mom's arms. *Bad idea, lady.* This only served to make my cries louder. There was no way I was letting go of my mom's neck. To the chagrin of Mrs. Thompson, and the embarrassment of my mother, I left room 107 with tears in my eyes. They quickly dried when I was back in the safe confines of our family station wagon. My initial foray into academia began the following day after my parents assured me I had nothing to be afraid of, especially the red carpet. I think I was finally convinced when my dad told me I was acting like a baby. *Baby? Timmy's a big boy.*

"Sorry, buddy, I have to go to class," Matt said as he he scurried out of the weight room like a death row inmate who had just received a pardon from the governor in the eleventh hour.

Matt's parting words snapped me back to reality. But, that same feeling of being left in an unknown environment I had experienced in Mrs. Thompson's class still lingered in my mind, as Matt left the weight room to go to math class. I thought of jumping into his arms and clinging to his neck as he walked out the door, but alas, I accepted my fate.

Without my lifting partner, I was left alone in the weight room as a stranger in a strange land. And, not unlike the main character in Robert A. Heinlein's book, *Stranger in a Strange Land*, I had to adapt to new surroundings. The main character, Valentine Michael Smith, is an orphaned child of the first manned expedition to Mars, who is raised by Martians before being brought back to Earth by a second expedition. He is a man in his twenties, and looks at everything on his new planet through the ignorant eyes of a baby and must learn how to become a human being. On that day in the weight room, I was Valentine Michael Smith, feeling my way through the exercises, not knowing what to expect next, and Carlo indoctrinating me to my new world of Notre Dame football. Further fueling the parallel, I suspected Carlo was actually from another planet, as evidenced by his total lack of compassion.

I was now alone with Carlo, and he made me do squats while holding 100-pound dumb bells. This again pushed my mental as well as my physical limits. I could not even see straight at this point, and my head continued to spin. The squats were followed by a Pandora's box of different exercises, most of which, were designed to fatigue my muscles until they failed. Finally, after I forced out my last rep, I was told the workout was over. *Thank you, sweet Jesus.* No sweeter words were ever spoken than when I was released from Carlo's prison.

As I left the Joyce Center weight room, I tried to not show Carlo any weakness, despite the fact that a cloud of nausea hung over me. But as soon as the door closed behind me, and Carlo was out of view, I began running to try and make it outside. I got as far as the lobby before I lost all the food I had eaten that day right there on the lobby floor.

After I had left my tribute, one of the hockey coaches walked out of an office and said, "Tough workout, huh?"

I mumbled something incoherent and walked out of the Joyce Center and into the sunlight. The sunlight only served to drain whatever energy I had left from my body. I had about a half-mile walk back to my dorm, but I could not even make it hundred yards before throwing up several more times on the lawn. I had to lie down in the grass because the dizziness was making it hard to walk without instigating another bout of vomiting. I laid on the grass for five minutes with my face pressed against the cool green earth before attempting to walk again. I made it another hundred yards before having to lie down and rest again. What should have been a five-minute walk back to my dorm, turned into a battle of attrition. Eventually I made it to my dorm and up the stairs to my room. When I arrived, I felt like I had conquered Mt. Everest. I don't think Rip Van Winkle ever enjoyed a deeper sleep than I enjoyed that day.

It was the hardest workout I had ever experienced in my life. I had harder ones after, but I knew more what to expect. My body eventually became conditioned and prepared to handle the shock to my system for which high school lifting had not prepared me. I did not think it at the time, but I'm grateful Carlo did not accept anything other than all I had. That day in the leg press is something I always remembered and, looking back, I'm glad it happened. It became something I could call on when things got tough and I felt discouraged. In my mind, if I survived that challenge, then nothing could break me. I made it a point from that day forward to make sure the weight room would never get the best of me. Indeed, that which had not killed me had made me stronger.

After that workout, I questioned whether or not Notre Dame football was for me. I did not know if I could physically handle what was required of me. Every person has two voices inside their head: The first voice tells us everything we are capable of doing, and the second voice is the high-pitched whiny voice that refutes everything the first voice says. I knew it was just the devil on my shoulder telling me, "You can't do it." I decided from that moment, I was going to do everything in my power to reach my goals while on the team. I was going to be able to look back at my time at Notre Dame and have no regrets about how hard I worked. This was the attitude I took with me during every workout, every practice, and with everything I did. A lack of effort was not going to prevent me from success. I would do all I could and leave the decision to play me up to the coaches. But, from my end, Notre Dame football was going to get all I had to give. I reached a point in my life where I achieved my dream. I was living out the dream and picture I had for my life from the time I was a little boy. Now that I was on the team I had to set a new goal. I never felt satisfied with just being on the team and putting the uniform on. I wanted to play.

After having some idea what to expect from that first workout with Carlo, my teammates and I embarked on the off-season the day we got back from Christmas vacation. Everything I did during the second semester of my freshman year was geared towards getting bigger, faster, and stronger. I followed a strict diet and workout schedule. A typical day, from a journal I kept, looked like this:

5:30 a.m.
Wake up (drink 32 oz. of water)
6:15–7:30 a.m
Morning workout in small groups
(immediately after workout, drink one protein shake and take one vitamin pack)
7:45–8:45 a.m.
Breakfast (six hard-boiled eggs, one bagel, one bowl cottage cheese, one bowl mini-wheats, one glass skim milk, two bananas, one glass water, one glass orange juice)
9:15–10:30 a.m.
Calculus II
11:00 a.m.–12:15 p.m.
Biology
12:30–1:30 p.m.
Lunch (two cans of tuna fish, no mayo, 32 oz. water)
2:00–3:15 p.m.
Theology
5:30-7:00 p.m.
Team conditioning. (immediately after workout, drink one protein shake)
7:15–8:00 p.m
Dinner (two cans of tuna fish, no mayo, 32 oz. water, glass of skim milk, two bananas)

8:15–10:00 p.m.
Homework/study
10:15 p.m.
100 leg lifts and 100 push-ups
10:25 p.m.
Bed

Because I was training so religiously, I never touched alcohol. I figured if I was building my body during the week, I was not going to tear it down on the weekends by joining in any drunken debauchery. In college, nearly all social engagements revolve around alcohol. Throughout my four years people got used to the fact I didn't drink, so they never pressured me. There were many nights when my friends went out drinking, and I stayed home and lifted weights or ran. It was not easy to make the sacrifice, but I figured the rewards for my hard work outweighed any good parties I might miss. I did not drink soda, indulge in any sweets like ice cream or cake, eat fried foods, and rarely ate pizza throughout my five years at Notre Dame. Everything I did during the off-season was geared towards getting myself physically ready for the coming year. I did not want to again be left off the one-hundred-and-five-person party list when fall camp rolled around.

The first spring of my freshman year was very physically and mentally demanding. I was still adjusting to college life from an academic stand-point, and I had to follow a strict lifting and conditioning schedule. As a walk-on I had two choices of what time I could lift: Either 6:15 a.m. or 6:15 a.m. After much deliberation, I settled on a time. For three months straight, I lifted every Monday, Tuesday, Thursday, and Friday at 6:15 in the morning. Often times I would be so tired during class it was a struggle to keep my eyes open, and I'd fall asleep. So, at night I'd have to go over what I should have learned during the regular class period. In addition to the morning lifts, we had conditioning three to four days a week in the evenings. I'd go to sleep early because I'd have to get up and lift the next morning. Occasionally, studying for a test kept me up all night, and I'd have to lift weights after a sleepless night. My roommate, Matt Murphy, and I were on completely different schedules. He was an engineering student and was usually up late finishing a lab. Something must have worked out though because he was my roommate all four years of college. He is now an officer in the United States air force. I could not be prouder of him.

Every year in early April, spring football starts. NCAA rules allow fifteen practices. Included in those fifteen practices are three scrimmages, among which is our annual Blue and Gold game where fifteen thousand people usually attend.

For a walk-on, the Blue and Gold game is your chance to show what you can do. Everyone plays in the game so you know going in you will at least get a couple of chances to try and do something positive.

But before the Blue and Gold game, we had two scrimmages with live tackling and officials. In the first scrimmage of the spring I did not get a chance to play, and I was discouraged. I asked myself, "How am I going to show what I can do if I don't get a shot?" Our second scrimmage was in the stadium with real Big Ten officials. It was the end of the scrimmage when I finally got the call to line up in the backfield. The ball was spotted on the twenty-yard line, and Coach Davie said we would have one series to try and score. If we scored, the offense won; if we did not score, the defense won. The quarterback called the play. It was a running play designed to go to the tailback. I was going to carry the ball in Notre Dame stadium! I had been waiting for this moment for a long time. The play developed, and I got a good block from my fullback, and I cut it outside. I saw an opening, and I was sprinting down the sideline to the end zone. I thought I was going to score, but was pushed out of bounds at the one-yard line. Matt Sarb tackled me before I could reach the goal line. (I told him the only reason he was able to tackle me was because he had more energy in his legs due to leaving Carlo's workout early to go to class.) On the next play they called the same play to the other side, and I scored my first touchdown in Notre Dame stadium. It was the only touchdown scored that day. I called my parents as soon as I got home. I remember the day in every detail because it was something that was important to me. I imagine no one else even recalls it, especially the coaches. But, at the time, I thought they were penciling me into the starting line-up.

The next weekend was the Blue and Gold game. My whole family was in attendance. I got to carry the ball for the first time in front of people in the stands. I finished the day with three carries for seventeen yards. It was the most yards per carry out of any of the running backs that day. I felt I had proven something that spring, and I thought I would be invited to fall camp when August rolled around.

At the end of spring practice, I had a meeting with my position coach where my overall performance during spring practice was evaluated. My running back coach, Desmond Robinson, had all positive things to say about how I performed. I asked him if I was going to be invited to fall camp, and he said I would not be. The entire coaching staff, depending on the needs at different positions, decides on the one hundred and five players invited to camp. I really could not understand the reasons I was not included, but I had no choice but to accept the decision. I went back to my dorm that night and felt very discouraged. I talked to my parents, and they told me to try and stay positive. I felt I had done everything in my power to earn a spot on the one-hundred-and-five-person roster and had fallen short.

Two days later I received a phone call from Coach Chmiel telling me he needed to speak to me. I went over to his office, and he had me sit down. He informed me there was a change of plans, and I was going to be able to attend fall camp. He told me to follow him down the hall because someone else wanted to speak to me. He led me into Coach Davie's office. The office of the head football coach at the University of Notre Dame is a special place. The sight of the wood paneled office adorned with football memorabilia awed me. Coach Davie was sitting behind the desk, and I sat down across from him.

He opened up by saying "I bet you were a heck of a high school running back."

What do you say to that? If you say, yes, you sound arrogant. If you say, no, you sound like you lack confidence. So I compromised and just shrugged my shoulders and smiled. Coach Davie told me he liked what he was seeing out of me during practice, and the coaching staff had decided to invite me to fall camp. He asked me about my family, my high school stats, and various other topics. The conversation with Coach Davie did wonders for my confidence and showed me the coaches did notice my efforts. I walked out of his office feeling on cloud nine. I was going to fall camp! As an added bonus, this meant I would finally get my own locker and I could retire from the visitors' locker room.

One of the negative things about me going to camp was two of my best friends, Matt Sarb, and Adam Tibble, who was the walk-on kicker who had attended camp the previous year, would not be going. They had been told it came down to numbers and they just did not have room at their positions. They would be allowed to join the team once school started in late August.

It is hard to stay positive when you receive the news you will not be going to camp. The players who do not attend fall camp are usually left out of the program, and in general, feel ostracized from the program. I experienced that roller coaster of emotion during a three-day span, so I knew what Matt and Adam were going through. I know it would have been easy for them to quit and stop all the sacrifice because of the setback. But they did not quit and joined the team once school started. It would prove to be one of the best decisions either of them ever made.

EIGHT

FALL CAMP

"I don't know why we are here, but I'm pretty sure that it is not in order to enjoy ourselves."

~ Ludwig Wittgenstein ~

After spending the entire summer working at my high school doing landscaping and maintenance during the day, and following a strict strength and conditioning program at night, I reported to fall camp on August 7. This was a full week earlier than most other Division I teams, because we were playing in a pre-season game, the Eddie Robinson Classic, against Kansas. My parents dropped me off at the football office, and I was given a key to the dorm room I'd be staying in the next two weeks. After signing in, I had my picture taken in a coat and tie for the program, and then settled into my temporary home in Keough Hall.

During the first two weeks of August, Keough Hall serves as the base camp for all football related activities. During the rest of the school year, it houses up to two hundred and eighty male students. But, during fall camp the dorm is an amalgamation of trainers, players, coaches, student managers, and support staff. The one hundred and five players occupy the first two floors, while all the trainers and managers stay on the third floor. Study areas are converted into makeshift film rooms, and the basement transforms into a fully operational training room. The back door of Keough Hall funnels into a massive white tent, erected to serve as a provisional locker room for the duration of camp. Behind the dorm, a short walk from our ad hoc living quarters, are the practice facilities. They include two regulation-sized football fields and an adequate expanse of land for conducting drills.

After settling into our new dwellings, the entire team, including the incoming freshmen, congregated for a team meeting in the press box overlooking the stadium. Coach Davie went over his expectations for the season and detailed what our agenda would be for the next two weeks. Our schedule would consist of a 6:45 a.m. wake-up call to a chorus of air horns, followed by mandatory breakfast. Breakfast would be followed by meetings. Meetings would be followed by a two-and-half-hour practice. Practice would be followed by mandatory lunch. Although Coach Davie did not expound on this, lunch, I later learned, was usually followed by a brief football-induced coma in which we got to sleep for an hour. Another meeting and film session would follow the football-induced coma. Meetings and film sessions would be followed by another two hour practice. Practice would then be followed by a mandatory dinner. Dinner would be followed by more film sessions and meetings and then lights out by 11:00 p.m. If this schedule sounds monotonous, well, it is. For roughly twelve to fourteen days, every college football player has to go through this sixteen-hour day of football practices and meetings in preparation for the season. After Coach Davie was done with his speech and breaking down our practice and meeting schedule, I couldn't wait to get out on the practice field.

I might not have been as excited to start if I had heard the story of a player under Coach Holtz who was experiencing his first college football two-a-day camp. I heard this story later, on a day when every part of my body ached, including my eyelids when I slept. Notre Dame used to conduct their fall camp at Culver Military Academy, about twenty-five minutes from the Notre Dame campus. This sequestered, no air-conditioned environment was a horrible place to be for two weeks for every football player who endured it. One freshman player could not take the mental and physical exhaustion of the monotonous practices. So, rather than pouring what little energy remained in his body into practicing, he focused on hatching an escape plan. Because Culver did not have sufficient laundry facilities to handle the soiled uniforms of the football team, every day the dirty laundry was transported by truck back to Notre Dame's campus to be cleaned, then returned the following day.

This process happened like clockwork on a daily basis. After the second practice of the day, the team managers loaded all of the jerseys into gray bins marked, "PROPERTY OF NOTRE DAME FOOTBALL." This player evidently memorized the loading pattern, and when the managers' backs were turned, he made his escape by jumping into a cart of dirty laundry and quickly pulling the uniforms over his head. He was rolled onto the truck and nobody even knew he was there. Once safely back on campus, he called his father to come pick him up—mission accomplished.

When I first heard the story, I couldn't imagine anyone being so desperate not to practice, that they would endure a twenty-five minute truck ride back to campus under a pile of sweaty Notre Dame football uniforms. After a few days of fall camp, I would have welcomed getting away, no matter what I had to sit in.

But before I experienced my first day of fall camp, we had "Media Day" obligations. Media day is when the team and coaches are made available to the media for the first time to discuss the upcoming season. It is also the day individual and team pictures are taken. After the pictures are taken, the team is divided by position and seated at tables around the field to sign autographs. Even though people didn't know who I was, I still was asked to sign hundreds of autographs. I was honored. I could now put to practice the signature I had practiced thousands of times on folders and notebooks. It was hard to decide which signature to pull from my repertoire of John Hancocks. *Do I use Tim, Timmy, or just my initials? Should I put #35 next to my name or below it?* Despite the fact the fans looked quizzically at my signature to decipher who I was every time I passed along a football, a mini-helmet, or program, it was still flattering to have people even ask for my signature.

Many of the fans carried with them a media guide for the players to autograph. The walk-ons and the freshman were never included in the media guide so it was always awkward when they handed you the guide and asked you to flip to your picture and sign. I developed many excuses for such a situation.

"Um, there must have been some mistake, I'll have to talk to the sports information director, should I just sign the inside cover?" was one of my favorites.

Or they would sometimes provide an excuse for me, "Oh, are you a freshman?"

I would just nod my head in agreement to save from having to say, "I'm a walk-on, and they don't include us in the media guide."

I didn't want kids backing away from me looking for the *real* players. After media day activities subsided, I was issued the clothes I would wear for the next fourteen days, and everything I needed to begin my first official practice of the 1999 season. I now had everything I needed to begin my Heisman run, even, finally, a pair of size 8 ½ cleats.

Day three of camp I began to wonder why I had been so excited to start. Since I was sequestered with my teammates and coaches and all of my energy and concentration was devoted to football, I began to feel like a zombie. The practices were fun, but all of the meetings and film sessions were difficult to get used to. Every play we executed and every drill we ran was filmed. Basically, everything we did on the football field was videotaped for later dissection. It felt like a reality TV show, except I didn't have my choice of a beautiful woman at the end of filming.

For every one drill or repetition I ran during practice, the scholarship players ran twenty. That meant there was a 20:1 ratio of opportunities to try and make a positive impression, so the value of every play a walk-on ran was magnified by twenty. The inherit disadvantage was also present during film sessions, when, after watching your teammates being coached, the few reps a walk-on got were usually fast-forwarded. So, as a walk-on, you had to know your plays through observation only, because you rarely had a chance to run them during practice, and when you did, you weren't always coached on what you needed to correct. This was just the reality of the situation, not an excuse. The players that had been recruited were given every opportunity to earn a seat at the table, while the walk-ons had to wait for the scraps. It was my intention to one day be invited to the feast.

It is difficult to navigate through the politics present in any organization, and Notre Dame football was no exception. However, it was not impossible to chart a course for yourself as a non-scholarship player. When I began as a fledgling football player attending my first fall camp, I looked to the upperclassman for motivation. There were four guys in particular I truly respected. My four idols were Anthony Brannan, Jonathan Hebert, Mike Zelenka, and Jeremy Juarez. Their work ethic and attitude served as an inspiration to me and was something I tried to emulate. Jonathan was a wide-receiver and played extensively on special teams. Anthony was a linebacker who would later earn a full scholarship. Mike was a linebacker and my lifting partner for two years. Jeremy was a fullback, whose hitting prowess was legendary. There weren't many people man enough to take on a block from Jeremy Juarez. His primary objective was to clear a path for the ball carrier. His secondary objective was to draw blood. These four guys never allowed doubt to creep into their psyches, and they never doubted their abilities. I saw how they carried themselves, and I wanted to follow in their footsteps.

By the fifth day of camp we settled into a regular routine being played out on numerous college campuses across the country. We'd get up at the crack of dawn and run drill after drill in the early August heat. There was always an interesting dichotomy between the time we were on the practice field and the time we were walking to and from practice. At practice, bodies flew around with speed and grace, but after practice the same people who looked invincible on the field could barely walk or looked pale from exhaustion. Every part of our bodies ached, and after every practice we would submerse our bodies in a 55-gallon drum filled with ice and water to help alleviate the pain from the previous practice.

Sometimes at night, instead of the usual football meetings, we would have self-improvement seminars. This gave us a chance to break the monotony of the practice/meetings, practice/meetings, cycle. On one such occasion the speaker handed out a piece of paper and had us write a letter to ourselves. We were to include our address on it, and then at some time during the season, she would mail the letter back to us. It was meant to organize our thoughts on paper and to set goals for the season. I gave my letter a lot of thought, but I had virtually forgotten all about it until I received it later in the season.

The subsequent days of camp began to meld together since I had no contact with the outside world. So, when school started, it was a welcome change of pace to see the campus begin to populate with nervous freshman and seasoned upperclassmen. We moved out of Keough Hall ten days after arriving, so the students who actually lived there could move in. I moved my belongings to my permanent residence in Stanford Hall, while my teammates dispersed to their respective dorms throughout campus. Notre Dame is unique in there is no housing specifically earmarked for athletes. Most schools have athletic dormitories where all the athletes are centralized. They eat together, sleep together, and socialize together. But at Notre Dame the athletes are scattered in different dorms and live with all the other students. This helps to acclimate the athletes to the general student body and vice versa.

On the day school started, my friends Matt Sarb and Adam Tibble started practicing with the team. They had to wait until school started to begin practicing, per NCAA rules. I know they felt slighted to not be able to join their teammates when fall camp started, because I had gone through that the previous year.

It was nice to have Adam and Matt back. These two, along with John Crowther, who had been invited to camp as a long snapper, and I, had become fast friends. We all essentially started at the same time, and we were able to commiserate with each other about the growing pains associated with learning how the system worked. I think we all fed off each other's positive energy. If one of us was frustrated, someone always knew what to say to reenergize the downtrodden party and remind them of their goals. We would definitely need this friendship to alleviate the disappointment of the coming season.

NINE

THE 1999 SEASON

"Show me a good and gracious loser and I'll show you a failure."

~Knute Rockne~

O n the night before we played Kansas, I experienced the Friday night pep rally I witnessed with my dad on my first annual trek to campus. It was held in the Joyce Center in front of twelve thousand people who were decorated in various shades of blue, gold, and green. The view I was privy to was considerably different than the one I experienced as a seven-year-old watching wistfully from the stands. My teammates and I sat on the floor of the basketball arena dressed in sport coats and ties as the crowd alternated between respectful listening and raucous undulations. The energy in the arena induced a rash of goose bumps, and there was no place I would have rather been at that moment.

The expectations among the Irish faithful were again high for the upcoming season. But this season, the excitement particularly transcended recent years because it was Bob Davie's third year at the helm of the program. The third year of the head football coach's tenure at Notre Dame had traditionally been the year they either stake their claim as a legend in the pantheon of college football or fail to meet expectations. Ara Parsegian won a national championship in his third year in 1966; Dan Devine won a title in his third year in 1977; and Lou Holtz claimed the title in 1988 in his third year. So the alumni expected nothing less than a national title in Coach Davie's third season, which, ironically, was 1999. The script was set up perfectly, and now it was up to the players and coaches to fill in the lines that would deliver a happy ending.

The season got off to a solid start with a 48-13 victory over Kansas in the Eddie Robinson Classic. It was a good tune-up game before we headed to Ann Arbor to play Michigan. As was tradition, the Monday after beating Kansas, the team enjoyed a victory dinner in the Joyce Center Monogram Room. During the victory dinner we feasted on a spread of steak and shrimp while watching the replay of the game that garnered the dinner. I would have gotten a third helping if I had known we wouldn't be eating steak and shrimp again anytime in the near future.

Unfortunately, the win over Kansas offered the only bright spot in the early part of the 1999 season. We lost our next two games on the road in heartbreaking fashion. We lost to Michigan after running out of time on the final drive of the game. Similarly, our loss to Purdue was as heartbreaking as a loss can be. We had the ball on Purdue's one-yard line as time expired. We were within inches of victory when we had a communication breakdown in the backfield, securing our second consecutive loss. Our quarterback called a dummy audible to try and confuse the defense, but it ended up confusing our backs instead, which led to a sack. With no timeouts remaining we could not get another play off before time expired.

The game was played at Purdue, so I watched the game on the TV in my dorm room since I was not on the travel squad. After the game I felt extremely frustrated. I was not even on the travel team, but the loss ate away at me. I hated losing, and I felt helpless because I could do nothing but watch the events transpire on television. After the game I had to do something or I was in danger of tearing up my dorm room, so I went for a run. My teammates were on a bus driving home from West Lafayette, Indiana, and running was the only thing I could think of that would positively channel my frustration. I will never forget running through the dark paths zigzagging through campus after having lost to Purdue. I could hear party music blasting from the windows of various dorms and muffled laughter emanating from the intimate gatherings as I ran by. I think it was then I realized my college experience was not going to be typical. My Saturday nights wouldn't be spent on a quest to see how much I could drink; rather, they would often be spent lifting weights or running. On the nights I did go out, I sometimes felt guilty I was not doing anything to get better. It is only in retrospect that I realize how neurotic I was. There really was not anything I did where football was not in the back of my mind.

Despite the disappointing start to the season, I thought I was starting to make strides on an individual basis. I was still running scout team tailback during practice, and I began returning kicks as our deep returner against our first team kick-off team. I got the job in large part because I just simply wanted it. I viewed it as my chance to prove I could run the ball. I repeatedly hung around and caught kicks while the coaches shuffled in different players to return kicks against our first team coverage unit. One day the coaches finally gave me a chance to return kicks (I think they eventually got sick of kicking me out of the drill and acquiesced).

Returning kicks during practice wasn't the most enviable job on the field. Basically the ball was kicked off and eleven guys tried to tackle me while I navigated through the humanity with the help of my blockers. I ran back a pretty good return during my first real opportunity to go against the first team. The next day during film sessions Coach Davie was looking at the tape and stopped it during my return to point out that he thought I was doing a "heck of a job."

Coach Davie always made it a point to show he appreciated my efforts, so I thought it was only a matter of time before I'd be seeing some real playing time. On one occasion, after practice was over, the entire team huddled on one knee around Coach Davie. This was typical protocol for the end of practice. He usually reflected on our effort during the day and gave us a rundown on any pertinent information we may need for the days ahead.

After we gathered around him he said, "Tiny Tim, I want you to stand up."

There was always one in every crowd, and this occasion was no exception, as after I had stood up, one of my teammates shouted from the back, "Tiny Tim, coach told you to stand up!"

This Napoleonic joke was met with laughter, before Coach Davie said, "I know some of you guys down there that are working with the offense don't get to see him run the ball, so I just want to point out to this football team that he's doing an incredible job."

It was probably the best compliment I had ever received. I felt Coach Davie showed a lot of confidence in me as a football player, and it did wonders for my own confidence.

The week prior to the Michigan State game, I was returning a kickoff during practice. I saw a lane to run through, and it looked like I had a clear path through the tacklers. As quickly as the hole opened up, it closed again when one of the tacklers appeared. One of our corners, Lee Lafayette, had "blown me up" as they like to say in the football vernacular. It was the hardest I had ever been hit in my life. Trying to show I was tough, I got right back up and moved on to the next drill. I carried the ball a couple of times against our defense before I realized my shoulder was numb. It turns out I had separated my shoulder and was told I would miss a couple weeks of practice.

During this time when my shoulder was separated, I could not practice. So at night I ran two miles around the two beautiful lakes on Notre Dame's campus. I could not swing my right arm because of the injury, so I'd run by only pumping one. Fortunately, after a week of no contact, I was able to begin practicing again. It still hurt, but the pain was now bearable.

The Michigan State game was almost a mirror image of our previous two games in we came up short in the final quarter. The previous week we lost to Purdue after being stopped inside the one-yard line in the final seconds. Two weeks before, we lost to Michigan when a last minute drive ended on the ten-yard line as time ran out. The Michigan State game didn't come down to the last drive of the game, but we entered the fourth quarter with the score tied 7-7. Both teams exchanged a pair of field goals in the final stanza, with our kicker, Jim Sanson, finishing the quartet of field goals to tie the score at 13-13 with 5:44 left in the game. But on Michigan State's next possession, Gari Scott caught an eighty-yard touchdown pass from Spartan quarterback Bill Burke to secure our third straight loss in as many tries. Our record stood at 1-3, only the seventh time in the previous 111 years Notre Dame had started with a similar record or worse.

A 1-3 record is completely unacceptable. At Notre Dame, it seems like a death sentence. The more success you have, the higher the standard becomes. That is how it should be. Notre Dame ranks at the top of college football with eleven national championships, seven Heisman trophy winners, and the most consensus all-Americans of any other school. So with a 1-3 record, we hit rock bottom.

The week after we lost to Michigan State, I was finding it hard to stay positive. Our record was abysmal and my shoulder was making just sleeping difficult. It was during this week I had a letter dropped off in my locker with the familiar envelope I vaguely remembered. It was the letter we had to write to ourselves during fall camp that was promised to be returned to us later in the season. The timing of the letter could not have been better, as I really needed a pick-me-up. I slowly opened the yellow envelope with the familiar gold triangle, and read the words I had written five weeks earlier:

Dear Tim:

I am making a promise to myself to never underestimate myself and my dreams and what I'm capable of doing. I've always said I believe through hard work and dedication anything is possible. I want to be able to look back at my years at Notre Dame and know that if I didn't achieve something, it wasn't because of a lack of effort. I realize I have a tremendous opportunity to get a Notre Dame education and to play football at the school I love. I will not sell myself short. In all things, I want to conduct myself with integrity and class. Whenever possible I hope God will help me to reach out to those who are less fortunate, and those who are doubting themselves and their dreams. I believe I have a special opportunity to put myself in a position to be successful, not only at Notre Dame, but the rest of my life. I still have many things I would like to accomplish, and my faith will see me through all things. In the future I want to have a successful job doing something I love, but more importantly, I want to be a good husband and father. I am thankful for my parents and siblings and for everything I've been blessed with.

P.S. "If it was easy, everybody would do it."

The letter really came at a much-needed time. It's amazing how reading one's own words can reenergize a person. I had been listening to the little voice inside my head that was telling me to feel sorry for myself instead of to the positive voice that knew good things were going to happen.

Following a bye week, we played Oklahoma and staged a great comeback victory. We rallied for a 34-30 win over number twenty-three ranked Oklahoma after facing a 30-14 deficit early in the third quarter. Our quarterback, Jarious Jackson, had a career day completing fifteen of twenty-one passes for 276 yards and two touchdowns while rushing fifteen times for 107 yards and a touchdown. It was a great win and an excellent job of coaching to defeat an Oklahoma team who would go on to win the consensus national title the following season. As a 1-3 football team, we could have easily folded after falling behind by sixteen points with less than a half to play, but we didn't.

One of the catalysts of our comeback was Joey Getherall, a 5'7", 165-pound, wide receiver who snagged six catches for 133 yards. Everyone liked to talk about his size, but he was one of the best receivers in the country regardless of stature. He had my unyielding respect because of his work ethic. I saw his attitude and approach to the game matriculate every day during practice. Of course, in my own mind, I made the size comparisons, but I never looked at him as anything other than a great football player. The challenge for me was always to try and get rid of the adjective. I wanted to be viewed as a good football player, not as a good *undersized* football player. Joey had successfully achieved that, and I hoped to follow his example.

We were preparing for our next opponent on the Monday following our victory over Oklahoma, when Coach Davie stopped me to ask me a question. During the preceding week of practice leading up to the Oklahoma game, I had some decent kick-off returns and Coach Davie must have noticed.

We had a slight break in between drills when Coach Davie said to me, "Tiny, how fast are you?"

"I guess that depends on who's chasing me, Coach," I replied

He smiled, and said, "I want to get you back there on a kickoff return. You think you could handle that?"

I assured him I could handle it and that was the end of the conversation. I didn't want to get my hopes up or read too much into our brief tête-à-tête, so I relegated it to the back of my mind, but I hoped Coach Davie would remember the exchange.

The following day Coach Davie had his weekly press conference to discuss our upcoming opponent, the Arizona State Sun Devils. During this address to the media, one of the reporters asked him about the role walk-ons play in the football program.

He had this to say, "We have a tailback, Tiny Tim, Tim O'Neill….I said to him the other day, I said, 'you know what, we're going to get you back there on a kickoff return,' because the guy every day goes out there and does an unbelievable job."

I didn't know he had made these comments until the next day at practice, when one of my teammates told me. Evidently he did remember our conversation, so I began to think an opportunity to play might be in the near future.

Our game against Arizona State was a convincing victory. Late in the fourth quarter we led 48-17, and I kept inching closer to the coaches in hopes my number would be called.

Arnaz Battle was at quarterback, and I heard Coach Davie say, "Where's Tiny Tim?"

I quickly appeared at his side, not allowing him any time to change his mind. Desmond Robinson, my running back coach, sent me into the game, and I lined up in the huddle. I was seconds away from realizing my dream. I was going to play tailback for Notre Dame! I lined up in the huddle, and I waited for Arnaz to call a play. Jeremy Juarez was at fullback, so I knew I was going to be well protected. Arnaz called an isolation running play where I was going to get the ball off the left tackle. I almost did not get the chance.

I had never run a play during practice while Arnaz was at quarterback. He was always with the offense, and I was always with the defense. Arnaz repeated the play twice in the huddle and then called out when the ball was going to be snapped.

Before lining up, he said, "On first sound, on first sound, ready, break!"

We broke the huddle, and I was prepared to execute the play as soon as Arnaz got up to the line.

I thought the ball was going to be snapped immediately when he said, "Hit!" because that is how I had rehearsed it hundreds of times during practice while running with the scout team.

But his cadence was a little different.

He said, "Set, 187, 187, Set, Hit!"

So, when he said, "Set," I thought the ball was going to be snapped, and I flinched.

Luckily for me the referee did not throw a flag for illegal procedure. If I ever meet that official, I'm going to thank him profusely.

My first play of my college career almost resulted in a penalty. My first carry I got the ball and gained two yards. But as soon as the tacklers piled off me I was looking at the side judge to see if there was a yellow flag on the field. *Phew!* There was nothing but green, beautiful grass. After that first carry everything calmed down in my stomach, and I imagined there was no one in the stands and it was just another practice. This is the moment I had been waiting for, and I was not going to let nerves get in the way. The next play was the same play we had just ran but to the other side. I saw an opening, but just as I was accelerating through the hole, a defensive lineman tripped me up. *Damn it!* I really thought I should have broken that one. There was only one reason to carry the ball, and that was to score a touchdown.

I finished my debut with two carries for four yards. I was honored to have been given a chance to play by Coach Davie, but I was disappointed I only gained four yards. Still, as a sophomore walk-on I had accomplished a lot. I had played and carried the ball. It was only the fifth game I had ever dressed for, so I felt I was definitely starting to reach my goal of contributing to the team in a more visible way than through my participation in practice. I thought since I played so early in my career I would have many more opportunities to show what I was capable of doing. I did not know it at the time, but I would not touch the ball for the next three years.

After the game I showered and went out of the locker room to meet my parents. Before I could make my way out of the stadium, six or seven reporters and a cameraman greeted me and started asking me questions with microphones and a bright light in my face. *Are you kidding me? I didn't do anything. I only had four yards.* It was still flattering to be getting that type of attention, but I did not feel I deserved it. I felt like saying, "Come back when I do something." But my parents witnessed it, and it was a thrill for them to see their son getting so much attention.

Thursday of the following week I got a note in my locker telling me I was supposed to meet with the NBC commentators after I was done with class. Pat Hayden and Dick Enberg of NBC interviewed me, along with Jonathan Hebert, who had blocked a punt against Michigan State. It was very flattering, and I thought, *If I'm getting this much attention for simply getting four yards then what's going to happen when everything finally clicks for me?*

Because of my size and because I was a walk-on, people looked at my situation as a fairy-tale type story. Anything you did positive as a walk-on stood out because people did not have high expectations for you. Anything you failed to do was because you were a walk-on, and they did not really expect much out of you anyway. I was constantly trying to fight that image. I looked at myself as a member of the Notre Dame football team. I held myself to the same standards as anyone on the team. That is why I did not like the fact I seemed to be getting attention simply because I was a walk-on. If a scholarship player would have gotten four yards on two carries people would not want to talk to him, and if they did, they would say, "What happened out there?" But with me, it was like, "Aren't you proud?"

After the Arizona State game, we won our next two games to bring our record to 5-3. Unfortunately, we lost our final four games and finished the season a dismal 5-7. We had won a national championship in 1966, 1977, and 1988, so in the minds of the Notre Dame faithful, we thought the cosmos would align and we would win another one in 1999. It did not happen as we would have liked, and many Notre Dame alumni were getting restless. They wanted our head coach fired. They reasoned he had three years to get the job done, and he failed to bring a national championship to the school. From the outside looking in, it was easy to make that assessment. Because Coach Davie had given me an opportunity as a sophomore walk-on, I did not agree with the general consensus. In my mind, he had enough confidence in me to give me a chance, so I was going to have enough confidence in him that he would lead us where we wanted to go.

TEN

ADVERSITY

"Sweet are the uses of adversity;
which as a toad, ugly and venomous,
wears yet a precious jewel in his head.

~William Shakespeare (*As You Like It*)~

Nothing brings a group of guys closer together more than adversity. Coach Davie held a team meeting as soon as we returned from Christmas break, and I think that is when each and every player rededicated himself to the collective goals of Notre Dame football. During times of disappointment it is human nature to look for someone to blame. The fans and the media found an easy target in Coach Davie. The head football coach at Notre Dame is one of the best jobs in the country when things are going well; when things aren't going well, the pressure is relentless. Everyone at the team meeting held inside the closed confines of the Loftus Center auditorium knew what people outside the program were thinking. As the negativity mounted, so, too, did the resolve to never allow another season like 1999 to ever happen again.

The off-season consisted of lifting and running almost every day, and on the rare days it wasn't required, I'd lift and run on my own. A typical day consisted of lifting at 6:15 a.m., class, then a team run at 6:30 p.m. The lifting sessions were always intense, and they required strict attendance. If you were late by even thirty seconds there was hell to pay—I learned the hard way one morning when my worst fear became a reality.

I had been up late studying for an accounting test the night before my typical morning lifting session. After retiring to sleep at 2:45 a.m., I knew the next morning was going to be a battle against fatigue. I diligently set my alarm clock for 5:45 a.m. and laid down for an abbreviated sleep. As my head hit the pillow I was equally worried about how I was going to survive my accounting test as I was about my morning workout. When I was roused from my sleep I looked over at my alarm clock, which stared smugly back at me, illuminating a grinning 6:15 across its façade. *Why have you failed me?* So many times it had awoken me from a slumber with its rhythmic buzzing, yet, sadly, today, it had let me down. It didn't take me long to do the math; unless I could transpose myself into the weight room instantaneously, I was going to be late. I thought about just going back to sleep since I was already late, but I got up, knowing I was going to have to pay the proverbial piper.

I ran to the weight room, thinking if I showed up breathing hard, the judge would show leniency. When I arrived I changed into my workout clothes as I watched the other players in my lifting group already warming up. I got no further than five steps towards joining my teammates when the strength and conditioning coach, Mickey Marotti, pointed to the door and told me to get out. I turned around and walked out like a scolded dog and waited outside the weight room door not quite knowing what to do. *Am I supposed to leave? Should I wait for further instruction?* My answer came quickly when Mickey came out of the weight room holding a two-by-four and pointed me to the hundred-yard turf field inside of Loftus. The two-by-four could only mean two things: I was going to get beat with it, or I was going to have to do board pushes. I figured there had to be some rule against beating players with two-by-fours, so I resigned myself to the fact I was going to have to do board pushes.

I had heard stories about the board pushes, none of which had a happy ending. I didn't need instructions; I knew what I had to do. Mickey placed the two-by-four on the goal line, and I placed both my hands on top of it and began driving the board with my legs as the board slid across the turf. In theory, it did not seem that hard, you simply had to push the board from one end of the field to the other without stopping. But theory doesn't always translate into practice, and my legs are testament to the fact it is not an easy exercise. Mickey loved the simple yet physically demanding exercises—whether it be board pushes, monster tire flips, wall sits, or pushing a van around an empty practice field—he never lacked creativity in doling out punishments. After three hundred-yard board pushes, I was allowed to finish lifting with my teammates, vowing to never again be late. It didn't matter why I was late; there was never a good reason. That night I bought a new alarm clock and always made it a point to set two just in case one abandoned me in my time of need.

In addition to our mandatory workouts, the team occasionally got together at midnight to run the stadium steps in order to build team chemistry. We did not want to experience another season like the one we had in 1999 and that was evident in everyone's dedication.

After a grueling off-season, we began spring football practice in late March. The first day of practice, I was entering through the player's gate in order to get into the locker room.

A security guard stopped me and said, "Sorry, son, this gate is only for Notre Dame football players."

Before I could speak up, another guard came to my aid and said, "It's okay, he's a manager."

Now, I have tremendous respect for the team managers and the job they do, but that comment added a lot of fuel to my fire. That was just one of the many stereotypical comments people made when they looked at my size and automatically made assumptions. On another occasion I was talking to a young lady at a party and one of my buddies thought he would help my cause.

He leaned over and said, "You know, Tim plays football."

Without hesitation she said, "Cool, what dorm do you play for?"

That quickly deflated any ego I may have been forming. I can find motivation in almost anything, so I let those innocent comments stick with me in every workout and every conditioning session I went through.

Spring football came and went. I had three carries for twenty-two yards in the annual Blue and Gold game, and I didn't have the uncertainty of wondering whether I'd be inv ed to fall camp. Matt Sarb and Adam Tibble, who had been left off the list the previous year, were also invited.

After the culmination of spring football practice, the students take their final exams. The majority of the student body heads home for the summer following finals week, but all of the scholarship football players stay on campus to take summer classes and train. This serves two purposes: The players are able to take a couple of summer classes, which, in turn, lightens the academic load during the football season (e.g., instead of having to take fifteen credits, they may only have to take twelve). And it also allows the entire team to lift weights and condition together in preparation for the upcoming season. I wanted nothing more than to stay in South Bend to be with my teammates for the summer, but as a walk-on, I needed to make money to help pay for school. So the summer before my junior year I went back home and took a job working forty hours a week at a steel plant near my house.

I worked for a company called Sennett Steel. It was the same place former Notre Dame football players Jerome Bettis and Rodney Culver had worked (both Detroit natives). The owner of the company, as well as five of his children, had graduated from Notre Dame.

My first day on the job he said to me, "You're going to learn how to do a job you'll never want to do again after this summer."

He was right. My job was to band the steel together to prepare it for shipping. I pried the steel up with a crowbar-like device and placed blocks underneath it so it could then be banded together with a banding machine. This was always a good shoulder workout. I also got the enviable job of grinding steel. To do this job, I had to wear a fiberglass mask that protected me from the sparks cascading off the steel pieces. Once the edges of the steel had been grinded, I stacked them for shipping. After work I was covered in a thin film of filth, my face was black, and when I'd blow my nose, black dust came out. It was a tough job, but I was grateful to be making some money for the upcoming school year. It also provided a job in which I was doing manual labor for eight hours instead of sitting behind a desk. That could only help to get me in better shape for the upcoming season.

I was usually exhausted after work, but if I went home and sat down I knew I'd never get up. Our strength and conditioning coach had given me a workout to follow over the summer, so every day after work, I went home, changed out of my filthy clothes, then headed to my high school track with my friend, Vinnie. Vinnie and I played high school football together before I headed off to Notre Dame and he left to play Division III football at Hope College. He was one of my best friends and was my lifting partner for the entire summer.

Vinnie and I made a pact to follow the workout in every detail, no matter the circumstances. Inclement weather would not interfere with conditioning, nor would being too tired from a long day of work. We alternated days of driving to go workout. On a few occasions I'd call Vinnie to go workout, and he wouldn't answer because he'd be sleeping—so I'd just drive over to his house and wake him up. The same scenario played itself out on occasion at my house. I'd come home from a long day of work with the intention of getting ready to work out, but before I could leave, I'd fall asleep—only to be awakened to the familiar beeping of Vinnie's car horn blasting in my driveway. Working out was our drug that summer, and we got our fix on a daily basis.

We traveled religiously to the quarter-mile track at Athens High School to complete the quickness and speed-training portion of our workout. To work on our sprinting starts, we started in a variety of different positions—lying face down, lying on our backs, in a push-up or sit-up position, kneeling or seated. One of us would give a signal to jump up and the other would sprint out of position as fast as they could. To improve our sprinting form, we rehearsed our technique at slow speeds and then transferred to runs at maximum speed. We used resistance training to improve our acceleration and explosiveness. I placed a padded strap that was attached to two eight-foot lengths of tubing with handles attached to the end around my waist. While I ran, Vinnie dragged behind me, providing resistance by holding the two ends of the tubing. After my sprinting set was over, Vinnie and I switched roles.

In addition to the speed training, we did agility drills and plyometrics to develop our change of direction and proprioceptive abilities. These drills included agility ladders to improve footwork and a myriad of other exercises to work on cutting and lower body control. We made these drills competitive by using a stopwatch to track our times and these became the source of bragging rights until the winner was dethroned. As a reward for completing the speed and agility training, we got to do our conditioning. This was always the most dreaded aspect of the workout because it was all strictly timed with predetermined rest intervals that never lasted long enough. These running sessions on the Athens High School track usually lasted an hour and half, and then we lifted weights, alternating days between upper and lower body.

Our marathon training sessions usually lasted until 7:30 p.m., which made for a long day. I worked from 6:30–3:00, went home and changed into my workout clothes, then went right to work out until 7:00 p.m. Vinnie and I were in the best shape of our lives, and I was confident I was doing everything I could to prepare myself for the upcoming season. I had gone from bench pressing 225 pounds seven times as a freshman to doing it eighteen times. At the beginning of the summer it was a struggle to complete eight 110-yard sprints under the allotted time, and by the end of the summer Vinnie and I were doing twenty 110-yard sprints with time to spare. All my work was geared towards one purpose—I wanted to be able to contribute and help my team win. It did not appear I would be getting a legitimate opportunity at tailback, so I focused my energy into earning a spot on a special team.

The tailback position was a logjam of talented players with Tony Fisher, Terrance Howard, and Julius Jones all ahead of me on the depth chart. There was no doubt these were talented players, as Tony and Julius would both eventually forge careers in the NFL, but I never allowed myself to acquiesce to any of them. It didn't matter if I was a fourth string tailback in everyone else's minds; I never viewed myself as less talented than any other running back. There were things I didn't do as well as the others, but I felt I did other things better.

If I ever believed in my heart I was not good enough to play and contribute, I honestly would have quit. This viewpoint may have been a product of my wonderfully delusional mind, but it kept me confident in my abilities. Even though I thought I could get the job done at tailback, the reality was, if I was going to see the field, it was going to be on a special team. I felt I needed to show the coaches I was in the best shape of my life when I returned from summer vacation. When August rolled around, in my mind, I was ready.

ELEVEN
DISAPPOINTMENT AND HOPE

"If you accept the expectations of others, especially negative ones, you will never change the outcome."

~Michael Jordan~

ichael Jordan's quote embodies one of the great tenants of life. If you ever allow yourself to be defined by what others think of you, then happiness will always be an abstract concept. Not only should you never accept other people's expectations of how your life should be, you should have a higher expectation for yourself than anyone else could ever imagine. Success should never be a surprise, and you should never be in awe when you eventually find yourself in the exact situation you dreamed about—after all, it was you who did the work to get there. Other people may call you lucky because they underestimated your ambitions, but success seems easy to those who weren't around while it was being earned.

Life is about expectations. If tomorrow is not going to be better than today, where is the motivation to push yourself to succeed? The carrot of expectations dangles in front of the collective eyes of everyone—and those who choose to chase it hope one day there will be a visceral payoff. Those who stay behind and choose not to chase the life they imagine may live very happy and fulfilled lives—but with one very important caveat. They will always have the "what if" factor hanging over their heads. *What if I would have flown to Los Angeles, waited on tables, and tried to one day see my name in lights? What if I would have asked that attractive stranger at the coffee shop if the empty seat next to them is taken? What if I wouldn't have dropped out of medical school because the course load became too demanding?* These rhetorical questions and others like them are posed in the silence of people's minds on a daily basis. I knew I would eventually have to play and rewind "what if" scenarios in my mind's eye if I didn't push myself as hard as I could. I was determined when it came to Notre Dame football I would have no regrets because I never wanted to have to look back and wonder, *What if I would have worked harder?*

We had a sign hanging up in our weight room that said simply:

PAIN OF DISCIPLINE
PAIN OF REGRET
TAKE YOUR PICK

If we were spending three hours of our day working out, it wouldn't make sense for us to not give it everything we had. However, it was still possible to go to the weight room and work out without truly pushing yourself past your mental limits. You could still get a good workout, but when you left the weight room, even if no one else noticed, you knew you could have given a little bit more. Arnold Schwarzenegger understood this concept perhaps better than anyone else when he said, "The last three or four reps is what makes the muscles grow. This area of pain divides the champion from someone else who is not a champion. That's what most people lack, having the guts to go on and just say they'll go through the pain no matter what happens." It made sense to me that if I was going to have to go through the pain anyway, I may as well choose the pain of discipline, so I wouldn't have to look back with the pain of regret weighing on my conscious.

Going into the 2000 football season, I was in the best shape of my life. I was no longer an underclassman, and I knew how the system worked. I felt if I could earn a starting job on a special team, I would be able to prove myself in that capacity, and that would lead to opportunities to play at tailback. The timeline I set in my biological clock was to learn as much as I could as a freshman, earn playing time in a clean-up role as a sophomore, then come to fall camp ready to really contribute as a junior. Unfortunately my timeline of events didn't coincide with what actually happened.

When the initial special teams depth chart was released during fall camp, I combed over the sheet looking for my name. I was nowhere to be found. I asked myself, "Have you done everything you could?" My honest answer to myself was, yes. At least if I felt I could have worked harder, it would have been easier to take. I felt I was being slighted because I was a walk-on and because of my size. Just because someone is a hard worker doesn't mean they should automatically be given the keys to the kingdom. There are a lot of hard workers in the world who don't measure up to their peers in terms of ability. But I truly believed in my heart I was not only capable of playing and contributing, but I would excel if given an opportunity. I guess I was hoping my confidence in myself would one day become its own self-fulfilling prophecy.

Although I felt I was stuck stagnant in a room without doors, I was encouraged by the progress of my teammates. Four of my walk-on friends earned starting jobs on special teams at the start of the 2000 football season. Chad Debolt, Matt Sarb, John Crowther, and Adam Tibble all earned first-team positions. I couldn't have been happier for them, and it made me even hungrier to keep working for my own opportunity.

Chad Debolt's first opportunity to play in Notre Dame stadium came in our season opener against number twenty-three ranked Texas A&M. After coming to Notre Dame to play Lacrosse, he walked on to the football team in the spring of our freshman year. He joined Shane Walton, a defensive back and former soccer star, as the only other player to earn letters in more than one sport. After playing scout team linebacker during our 5-7 season, Chad was able to impress the coaches enough to earn a starting job on the kickoff and punt block teams at the start of the 2000 season. His debut coincided with our impressive 24-10 victory over Texas A&M.

The victory was crucial to our fledgling season and gave confidence to our quarterback, Arnaz Battle, who was making his first collegiate start. He answered many of the questions about his ability to lead our team to victory by completing 63 percent of his passes and throwing two touchdown passes. The consensus in the locker room and among the coaches was very optimistic for the prospects the rest of the season with Arnaz at the helm. This confidence was infused at a pivotal time as we prepared to play the number one team in the country.

The number one ranked Nebraska Cornhuskers were thirteen and a half point favorites when they journeyed to South Bend. Eight-hundred twenty-one media members attended the game to witness Nebraska's Heisman hopeful quarterback, Eric Crouch, battle the most storied program in college football. The hype surrounding the game was massive; so much so, the Friday night pep rally had to be moved to the football stadium because the twelve-thousand-person capacity of the basketball arena wasn't enough to house all the fans that wanted to attend. Despite being a two-touchdown underdog, the game exceeded all the hype and expectations.

When I came out of the tunnel during warm ups with my team-mates, it felt like we were walking into an away game atmosphere. The Nebraska fans had infiltrated Notre Dame stadium and secured over twenty-five thousand seats—which meant twenty-five thousand various shades of red dotted the stands. The Nebraska fans were known for traveling well, but this was an unprecedented display of fan support; as a player, it was disheartening to know many of our fans had sold their tickets to the enemy. Since Nebraska had only been allotted four thousand tickets by the University, the Nebraska faithful had done a noble job of finding a way to get tickets—some selling for as much as $750 per seat. As if playing the number one team in the country didn't carry enough challenges, our home field advantage was essentially neutralized because of Nebraska's loyal following.

The game was a seesaw battle in the first half with Nebraska holding a 14-7 lead when both teams headed for the locker room. But in the second half, Nebraska started to pull away when I-back Dan Alexander broke loose for a twenty-eight yard touchdown run to give Nebraska a 21-7 lead. It looked as though everything that was said by some of the Nebraska players during the week leading up to the game about Notre Dame's mystique not being a factor was prophetic. But, then it happened. In front of 80,232 people, the legends of Notre Dame were awakened for a brief moment on that fall afternoon.

After the game, a Nebraska defensive tackle said about playing at Notre Dame, "There is something; you can feel it here. You try to play it off as best you can, but there is something to it. This place is crazy."

The craziness began with 8:47 to play in the third quarter. After Nebraska scored to go ahead 21-7, the ensuing kickoff was fielded by Julius Jones and returned one hundred yards for a touchdown. Pandemonium broke out on the sideline as he raced by, and the momentum started to swing our way. On Nebraska's next possession, they were forced to punt to our always-dangerous punt retuner, Joey Getherall. After making a move on a defender no human should have been able to execute, Joey raced eighty-three yards for a touchdown. In a span of less than eight minutes, our special teams had exploded for fourteen points and ignited the passion of the entire stadium.

In the final stanza, neither team could manage any legitimate scoring drives and time expired with the score tied 21-21. No number one ranked team since Purdue in 1968 had left Notre Dame stadium with a victory, so going into overtime it seemed we had destiny on our side. In the extra period, we got the ball first and had to settle for a 29-yard field goal by our kicker Nick Setta to take a 24-21 lead. But on Nebraska's next possession, Eric Crouch scored the game-winning touchdown on a seven-yard dash around the left end to drive a stake through our heart. It wasn't supposed to end this way. I watched in stunned silence as the Nebraska players celebrated in the north end zone in the exact spot I envisioned our own celebratory scene playing itself out. We went back into the locker room feeling physically sick, knowing how close we came to vindicating much of the pain from the previous season.

The game was bittersweet for my lifting partner, Matt Sarb. We lost the game, but he realized a lifelong dream by playing in his first ever game in Notre Dame stadium. As a backup on the kickoff team, he had to be ready to play in case the starter in front of him went down. Following Julius Jones' one-hundred-yard kickoff return, Courtney Watson, our starting linebacker, was on the sideline fighting to catch his breath. Matt was Courtney's backup on the kickoff team and when he couldn't go, Matt got his opportunity. It was supposed to just be a cameo appearance while the starter rested, so Matt knew he had to make the most out of it—and he did.

With a national television audience watching, Matt ran down the field and completely decimated two Nebraska blockers with a hit so ferocious, it was replayed several times on NBC for the entire country to watch. I swelled with a tremendous amount of pride to see my teammate and friend achieving his goals. He was one of the first players to congratulate me after I played in my first game, so I was waiting for him on the sideline when he came off the field. With only one play to prove himself, he etched his name into the starting lineup and wouldn't relinquish the starting job on the kickoff team the rest of his career. If he wouldn't have spent all week watching film to know what he was supposed to do, or if he would have been too nervous in front of eighty thousand people to properly execute his assignment, he likely would have never seen the field again. As it was, he seized his moment in the spotlight and would never have to look back on his Notre Dame career with regrets—all because he was ready when the opportunity came.

On Sunday, still feeling the sting from the previous day's defeat, Coach Davie called an emergency team meeting. We knew something must have happened. On the first play of the game our starting quarterback, Arnaz Battle, had broken his wrist. Despite this, his adrenaline and courage allowed him to play the entire game without ever complaining of pain. No one even knew he was hurt until after the game when he allowed the doctors to examine him. After a thorough X-ray, the diagnosis was grim: our starting quarterback would miss the rest of the 2000 season. Furthering our early season disappointment, one of our captains, Grant Irons, also suffered a season-ending shoulder injury against Nebraska. Everyone in the team meeting knew the next week of practice would be critical, as we had less than a week to prepare our backup quarterback, Gary Godsey, for a high-powered Purdue team led by all-American quarterback, Drew Brees.

Much of the talk during the week leading up to the Purdue game revolved around how our 6' 7" sophomore quarterback would deal with the pressure of starting in his first collegiate game. Since the last game Godsey had played was as a high school senior in Tampa, Florida, questions circulated about how he would fare on the grandest stage in college football. But a sign hanging out of a dorm room on the north end of campus left little doubt who the student body supported. Written in thick black letters, and hanging from a bed sheet billowing in the wind, were the words, "IN GODSEY WE TRUST."

That trust would be severely tested with 3:39 remaining in the fourth quarter when Purdue catapulted to a 21-20 lead, following a twenty-two-yard touchdown reception by wide receiver Vinny Sutherland. But our sophomore quarterback proved to be undaunted by the magnitude of the situation and focused on what needed to be done. In an impressive final drive, Godsey completed four of six passes for thirty-eight yards. On a pivotal third and three, Julius Jones had an eight-yard run to place the ball on Purdue's twenty-two yard line with enough time on the clock to attempt a game-winning thirty-seven-yard field goal.

I laid down on my stomach on the sideline after saying a quick prayer with my teammate Eddie O'Connell (I figured a Hail Mary by two good Irish Catholics might help our chances). The game came down to one play and essentially was placed in the hands of three players: John Crowther, our snapper; Adam Tibble, our holder; and Nick Setta, our kicker. The previous week Matt Sarb had gotten his moment in the spotlight and now it was my walk-on teammates John Crowther and Adam Tibble who would help determine the course of the rest of our season. In the most pressure-packed situation a snapper, a holder, and a kicker can find themselves, they did not crack. The snap was perfect, the hold was perfect, and the kick sailed through the uprights. I ran onto the field with my teammates and hugged Setta as a juvenescent celebration ensued. The scene was in stark contrast to the somber atmosphere of the previous week.

Only a little over a year had passed from the time Matt Sarb and Adam Tibble had been told they wouldn't be included on the one-hundred-and-five-player roster to the one week span when they both found themselves in incredible circumstances no one will ever be able to take away. It is a tribute to their positive attitudes and perseverance they never allowed setbacks to block the path to their goals. I know how disappointed they were when they found out they wouldn't be going to camp, so to see them having success proved what a difference a year can make and what can happen when you refuse to become discouraged by your current situation.

John Crowther had his own unique story. A little over two years before becoming our starting snapper on field goals and extra points, he was content to be playing inter-hall football for his dorm team. He enrolled at Notre Dame with no intention of walking on to the varsity team but one phone call changed the course of his college experience. Unbeknownst to Crowther, his inter-hall coach had called the varsity coaches and gotten Crowther a tryout. After impressing the varsity coaches with his snapping abilities, he received a phone call inviting him to walk on. Not only was he going to be on the team, but he was going to be on the travel squad because the backup snapper had gotten hurt. So in a whirlwind three-week period, he went from an anonymous freshman student, to an anonymous member of the varsity football team. Instead of eating pretzels in front of a television set in a crowded dorm room and watching the Irish play on TV, he was going to be living the dream of thousands of little boys by even suiting up for the Fightin' Irish. Little did he know two years later he would be the launching pad for a game winning field goal in front of eighty thousand fans.

Chad DeBolt, Matt Sarb, John Crowther, and Adam Tibble were four of the most impressive people I had the pleasure to know. It is usually no coincidence when good things happen to good people who work hard. Sarb, Crowther, Tibble, and I had all started at essentially the same time, and DeBolt joined the team a few short months later. They were beginning to taste the fruit of their labor while I was still waiting to sample the sweet nectar. The fact we shared such a strong friendship made it easier to deal with the disappointment that I was the only one among us who wasn't playing on Saturdays. It was hard to practice every day, knowing on game day I wouldn't have an opportunity to influence the game.

Following our last second victory over Purdue, we traveled to East Lansing, Michigan, to play the Michigan State Spartans. After falling behind 20-7 late in the third quarter, we staged an impressive comeback to take a 21-20 lead with 7:59 left to play in the game. Because I was not on the travel team, I made the three-hour trip to the game by car and had a nosebleed seat in the upper deck. The players who were not on the travel team got free tickets to the away games, but this magnanimous offer was rarely accepted. If I wasn't traveling with the team, I preferred to sit in the silence of my room and watch the away games on television—I didn't like sitting in the stands while my teammates were down on the field playing. But since I had close friends who attended Michigan State, I decided to make the trip. By the end of my weekend journey I wished I had never left South Bend.

I had a bipolar experience from my vantage point in the upper concourse of Michigan State stadium. After we took the lead in the fourth quarter, I was an exuberant schoolboy giving high fives to complete strangers. I thought we were on our way to a 3-1 record with our only blemish an overtime loss to the number one team in the country. Life was good. Our three-year losing streak to the Spartans was finally going to be halted. My vision of our victory was further enforced when Michigan State faced a desperation fourth-and-ten in their own territory with less than three minutes remaining. I knew all we had to do was stop them on their next play, and we would win the game.

The next ten seconds passed in a macabre blur I will never forget. On Michigan State's fourth down play, we called an all-out blitz to put pressure on Michigan State's true freshman quarterback, Jeff Smoker. The blitz had been working for us all game—until that play. To my horror, Smoker calmly recognized the blitz, took a three-step drop, and fired a slant pass to wide receiver, Herb Haygood, who raced sixty-eight yards for a backbreaking touchdown. I felt the blood rush out of my face and the air come out of my chest as the Michigan State fans erupted around me. I didn't want to believe what I had just seen, but the demoralized feeling in my stomach and the screaming green and white clad fans forced me to face the truth—Michigan State had beaten us for the fourth straight year. I walked out of the stadium dejected, not knowing the Phoenix that was Notre Dame football would rise from the ashes of Spartan stadium in the coming months.

TWELVE

SEVEN IN A ROW

*"The best place to find helping hands
is at the end of your own arms."*

~Confucius~

In a four-week span we experienced a twisting, loop-to-loop roller-coaster ride of emotion. Two euphoric wins and two last minute losses left us with a 2-2 record and two weeks to prepare for our next opponent, the Stanford Cardinal. The paradigm we had been operating under for the previous eight months of an undefeated season and a national championship had shifted. We had to set a new goal because of the early season adversity and that meant setting our sights on finishing the regular season with seven straight victories. The redeeming quality of adversity is that it allows lessons to be learned that under normal circumstances would go untaught.

During the bye week, the team remained upbeat and confident. We had only won half our games, but we felt we were a couple of plays away from being undefeated. With an extra week to prepare for our next opponent, the coaching staff decided it was time to insert a new starting quarterback into the lineup. Gary Godsey had done an excellent job of providing leadership, but our coaching staff felt our offense would run smoother with a quarterback who was more accustomed to running an option offense. So we turned to a true freshman named Matt LoVecchio to be the third starting quarterback of our young season. Only a few months removed from his senior prom, he was forced into a difficult situation. We would find out during the final seven games how LoVecchio would respond.

On the Tuesday before we were to play Stanford, I was showering in the locker room after a full-padded practice. One of the managers came up to me as I was toweling off to say Coach Davie wanted to speak to me. This was not normal. I tried to recollect any classes I may have skipped that would warrant a meeting with the head coach. *Could he have found out I slept through government class?* No, I had my hat pulled down too far for even the teacher to notice. I was hoping for some good news. There weren't a lot of positives to keep me going when I wasn't playing. As I was walking back to my locker, I saw Coach Davie waiting for me.

He pulled me aside and said, "I want you to speak at the pep rally on Friday night. Will you do it?"

I was honored. It had not been that long ago I witnessed these Friday night rituals from the stands with my dad.

After I accepted, Coach Davie told me how the night would proceed, "I'm going to say a few words and then I'm going to introduce you. You can talk about your experiences, what Notre Dame football means to you, heck, you can talk about whatever you want." He then jokingly added, "Just don't get nervous now, there'll be twelve thousand people there."

Following practice I was eating dinner in the dining hall and one of our captains, Anthony Denman, came up to me and said, "Speaking at the pep rally on Friday, eh?"

I asked him how he knew, and he said Coach Davie had asked him who he thought should speak, and he recommended me. I went against Anthony every day during practice because he was our starting inside linebacker. More than once he had knocked my head off. In fact, he was the linebacker who made my eardrum ring on my second ever college carry. I respected how hard he worked and his leadership. So to have him tell the head coach he thought I should speak at the pep rally really meant a lot to me. Only two players are selected to speak before every home game and usually a special guest—Wayne Gretzky, Dick Vitale, and Dusty Baker were a few that spoke during my tenure—so I knew it was special to be asked to address the Notre Dame congregation.

The night of the pep rally I got up in front of a capacity crowd in the Joyce Center and spoke about what Notre Dame and football had meant in my life. The first thing I did after taking the podium was to have my parents stand up and be recognized, because I knew without their support I wouldn't be in the fortunate position I found myself every day.

I closed my speech by saying, "Whether you're a scholarship player or a walk-on, it doesn't really matter. It is how hard you are willing to work that will determine your future."

I believed that statement with every fiber of my being, and I would spend the next two years of my life trying to prove it.

After we beat Stanford at home, we traveled to play Navy in the Citrus Bowl in Orlando, Florida. This game was always played at a neutral site because Navy's home field did not have enough seating capacity to meet the ticket requests for the game. The week of the game, I found out I was going to be on the travel team for the first time in my career. It felt good to finally see my name on the list after so many times of combing over the sheet to no avail. I hadn't done anything different during the week of practice to earn a spot on the seventy-two-member travel team; I think Coach Davie just wanted to reward my work ethic. This was a source of mixed emotions. Of course I was glad to have made the travel team for the first time, but I also knew the only reason I made it was because the coaches wanted to reward me for being a hard worker.

As much as I appreciated and was honored to be asked to speak at a pep rally and to have made my first travel team, I always wanted the reward for my performance in practice to be playing time. I think any football player will tell you the reason they put in all of the work in the off-season and make constant sacrifices is because they want to be able to prove their worth on the football field. To me, I measured my success at Notre Dame by how much I played, so all the peripheral things, while thrilling and at times unbelievable in magnitude, left me with a void in my heart. That is not to say I was ungrateful, because those opportunities I was given off the football field are some of the things I look back on and treasure the most, but at the time, all my energy and focus was on getting onto the field.

Our trip to Orlando was a unique experience for me. We chartered a jet, and the only people on the plane were coaches, players, and the hierarchy of administration, including the president of the University, Fr. Edward "Monk" Malloy, and our athletic director, Dr. Kevin White. The prime rib and shrimp made for a nice in-flight meal before we touched down in Orlando after a two and a half hour flight. After landing we took three buses to Disney World for a brief buffet. The entire team was dressed in coats and ties so there was no shortage of people whispering among themselves as the massive linemen walked amid the children admiring Goofy and Mickey Mouse. Our stay in Disney World was brief, because with good reason, the coaches wanted us concentrating on the game. But I still had enough time to do some walking around and get my picture taken with someone whom I'd had a crush on since my childhood—Minnie Mouse.

My roommate at the hotel was our starting fullback, Tommy Lopienski. Since we had flown to Orlando on a Thursday, and our game wasn't until Saturday, a handful of us went down to the pool and splashed around the landscaped waterfalls at the hotel pool before our first team meeting. *So this is what they do on away trips.* This trip wasn't a typical experience because the team usually arrived at away games the night before and didn't participate in any fun activities—it was usually all business. Since the University was on its annual fall break, we would not be missing any classes by arriving in Orlando a day earlier than usual. Aside from the brief Disney World excursion and the even briefer dip in the pool, the rest of the trip was indeed, all business. Individual and team meetings occupied most of our time as we put the finishing touches on our game plan.

The game was a convincing 45-14 victory. From the sideline I watched our lead mount, and I felt I might get an opportunity to get into the game. My feeling was realized with less than five minutes remaining in the game when I got the call to go in, but not in the capacity I had thought. I was on the sideline and I saw our receiver coach, Urban Meyer, who is, at this writing, the head coach at the University of Florida, turn around and tell me to get into the game. I never played receiver before, so Coach Meyer told me where to line up and what to do on every play. In the locker room celebration after the game, I found Coach Meyer and thanked him for giving me the opportunity to play in the Citrus Bowl. He was probably the most intimidating coach on the staff and some of the stories I could tell about him would be enough to make a grown man cry. But I respected him, because if a player worked his tail off, he would give him an opportunity.

The Navy game was the only game I played in during the 2000 season. Fortunately the sting of not playing was alleviated by the salve of being in the midst of a winning streak. With Matt LoVecchio as our starting quarterback, we went on a magical run of seven straight victories—downing in succession: Stanford, Navy, West Virginia, Air Force, Boston College, Rutgers, and Southern California. The winning streak brought our season record to 9-2 and earned us an invitation to the Fiesta Bowl in Tempe, Arizona. It was the first time since the inception of the Bowl Championship Series (BCS), Notre Dame had been invited to one of the four major bowls. After our early season setbacks, the coaches and players rebounded valiantly. Not only was it an honor to be invited to the Fiesta Bowl, it also contributed a $13 million paycheck to the University. Since Notre Dame had no conference affiliation, any money received from post-season play was retained and the kitty didn't have to be split with any other schools.

One of the highlights of this winning streak was a game at home against a feisty and disciplined Air Force squad who staged a late game rally after we surrendered an eighteen-point fourth quarter lead. With enough time on the clock to execute one final play, the game was tied 28-28. The season, and our hopes of a major bowl bid, hung in the balance as Air Force lined up for a game-winning twenty-eight-yard field goal attempt. My face contorted in anguish as I witnessed a perfect snap and a perfect hold. The play seemed to elapse in slow motion before I closed my eyes and decided to let the crowd tell me whether or not our major bowl dreams had ended. But before the crowd could relay the outcome to me, I heard a loud "THUMP!" I looked up and saw my teammates jumping around on the field in a jubilant melee. While my head was bowed and my eyes closed, our junior safety, Glen Earl, had done the improbable—the loud thump I had heard was Earl blocking the game-winning field goal to force overtime. With his late game heroics, Glen Earl earned the moniker "The $13 Million Man," because we went on to beat Air Force in overtime, and the win allowed us to eventually secure a spot in the Fiesta Bowl and the $13 million pay day. I had a philosophy class with Earl so I asked him the following week what it felt like to be called "The $13 Million Man."

He responded in his typical congenial, witty style, "It feels good, but I still haven't seen a dime of that money."

From a team standpoint, I could not have been happier with our regular season, aside from the two losses. But from an individual standpoint, there were nights when I'd cry myself to sleep. I enjoyed the time with my teammates, and I loved being a part of Notre Dame football, but my frustration mounted on a daily basis. I questioned whether all the work I was putting into football was really worth it. *What was the point of sacrificing on a daily basis if there wasn't going to be a reward?* It didn't seem to matter what I did on the practice field or during the off-season, and this was a source of great personal frustration. I knew there were a lot of people who would trade places with me, and I realized how lucky I was to be living out a childhood dream. But at the same time, I thought there was more I could contribute, and I didn't think I was being given a fair chance to prove myself. When I enrolled at Notre Dame, I honestly felt I would be playing. If you would have told me through three years of blood, sweat, and tears I would have played less than five minutes, I don't know if I could have done it.

I know some readers may be thinking, "You were a 5'6" walk-on, what did you expect?"

I can understand how some may think that, but I have the advantage of being able to see the world through my own eyes. I knew some people looked at me and didn't expect much out of me because I was undersized and that was probably my biggest motivator. Every day I tried to let my play speak for itself. All one can ask for in life is an opportunity, and I thought my play in practice and my performance in the off-season warranted an opportunity. I didn't think when I started fall camp my junior year I would be anointed the starter, but I also did not think freshman scholarship players should be getting reps ahead of me in practice. I just wanted to be invited to the party; I wasn't asking to be the guest of honor.

During practice for the Fiesta Bowl, I was running with the ball and, as I was getting tackled, I reached the ball out to try and squeeze another yard out of the run. When my arm hit the ground I felt a shooting pain in my upper left arm that felt like I was being stabbed by a hundred tiny knives. I later found out I had injured my bicep tendon. I didn't even know what a bicep tendon was, but it was the worst pain I had ever experienced. I could barely lift my arm straight up from the side of my body. Whenever I used my left arm to stiff-arm, brace my fall, or raise it above my shoulder, I experienced a shooting pain in my upper arm. But I knew I'd have the next three months to rehab my injury, so I continued to practice in preparation for the Fiesta Bowl.

During this week of preparation, I received a note in my locker from our media director. The note said Curry Kirkpatrick from ESPN wanted to do an on camera interview with Matt Sarb and me. The feature was going to focus on how we both always wanted to play football at Notre Dame and on the history our families shared with the University. So, the next day, after class, we both went into a room inside the Notre Dame press box that had been converted into a TV studio—complete with lighting effects and a special backdrop. After the makeup artist made us look good (Matt needed more help than me), we answered questions from Curry Kirkpatrick while the camera rolled. Following an hour of questions, we were driven to the College Football Hall of Fame with Curry Kirkpatrick and the cameraman. Once there, we were filmed looking at the various Notre Dame football displays. We were told the feature was going to run the day of the Fiesta Bowl on ESPN's Bowl Championship Game preview show.

It was interesting to experience what goes into the special features I had watched so many times as a kid on ESPN. It was even more interesting for me to have anyone actually want to film me while I talked. And while it was fun for me to have the experience, I always dreamed about having a special feature done on me because of what I had accomplished on the football field, not because I had simply made the team, or because my family had a long tradition with the University. I was honored and I appreciated being given an experience not many people get to have, but, it really didn't mean anything to me at the time. I just wanted to play.

On December 22, we were allowed to leave campus to spend Christmas with our families. I spent three days back in my hometown of Troy, Michigan, before flying out to Tempe, Arizona, on Christmas night to join my teammates. We had a week of practice at a local Arizona high school to implement the final phases of our game plan before heading into Sun Devil stadium to play the Oregon State Beavers.

The game was a night game and the darkness surrounding the stadium mirrored the mood in the locker room following a lopsided defeat. The game was a disaster and all of the momentum of our seven-game win streak came to an abrupt halt in a 41-9 drubbing. It was one of the most humiliating nights ever for our program and only a late touchdown prevented the game from being our worst defeat in twenty-four bowl appearances. We had a lot of work to do in the coming months.

THIRTEEN

A LOT OF HART

*"I learned that if you want to make it bad enough,
no matter how bad it is, you can make it."*

~Gale Sayers~

fter the Fiesta Bowl, the off-season began in earnest. Coach Davie held a meeting when the team returned from Christmas break to establish our off-season goals and to discuss the direction of the program. One of the items on the meetings agenda was a new leadership council. Coach Davie wanted to establish a leadership council to provide a link between the head coach and the players. The leadership council was to be made up of three players from each class, and it would serve as a liaison between the team and the coaching staff to voice concerns before they became bigger issues. Before we left the meeting the student managers passed out paper and pens and each player voted for the three players from each class they wanted on the leadership council.

The next day, following a conditioning session, our strength coach, Mickey Marotti, relayed the names of the fifteen players who would make up the council. When I heard my name read I was honored. It meant a lot to me to know the people I cared about and respected the most voted for me. It provided validation for me all of the work was not going unnoticed by the people who knew me the best. My teammates were my family, and I held their opinions in the highest esteem.

The good feeling I got by being voted onto the leadership council was mixed with the frustration I felt because of the injury I sustained during preparation for the Fiesta Bowl. It was preventing me from doing a lot of the things I wanted to do. My arm prevented me from attacking the workouts with 100 percent intensity, and I felt like an invalid when I saw my teammates doing everything I wished I could do. It was hard to go into the weight room and not be able to bench press and only be able to lift with my right arm. Every morning before classes I went to the training room inside the stadium and got treatment. These sessions usually consisted of alternating hot and cold treatment as well as using ultra sound and electric pulse therapy to help facilitate the healing process.

After a month of this treatment I did not notice any significant improvement, so our head trainer, Jim Russ, had an MRI performed. The results were encouraging; I only had a slight tear of my bicep tendon, and I would not need surgery. I continued to get treatment and eventually was able to start bench pressing again with the use of a block attached to the bar that stopped the weight six inches from my chest. This allowed me to ease back into lifting heavy weight without putting the stress on my arm of bringing the weight all the way down to my chest. Slowly I began to regain my strength, but I did not return to my pre-injury strength for almost a year.

I was feeling pretty depressed during the spring of my junior year because of the injury. I wanted to push myself so much harder than my body was allowing me. But during this time I received a letter from a fourteen-year-old boy in Pennsylvania that got me out of my funk.

The letter was from a boy named Jonathan Hart, and he was from Wilkes-Barre, Pennsylvania. He wrote to me saying he had seen me play in one of the spring games. He explained to me his grandmother had recently passed away, and he was considering quitting football. His grandmother was his rock, his everything. She attended all of his games and was really an integral part of his life. He wrote to me asking for some advice. I think he was just searching for a mentor.

After receiving that letter, I had never felt more honored in my life. It really put things in perspective for me—that I was able to affect someone I had never met in a positive manner. It showed me what a platform I had in Notre Dame football and how, by just doing the right thing, I could impact someone's life in a small way. I had been feeling a little down because of the injury and because I wasn't playing, but here was a result more profound than any I could have imagined.

I wrote back to Jonathan after receiving his letter, and I just spoke to him from my heart. I told him I was sorry about the passing of his grandmother, but she would always be there with him. He now had an important guardian angel not everyone else had. I told him about how frustrated I had been at times with football, but the best decision I ever made was to stay with it. I told him if it were easy, every one would do it. I sent out the letter about a week after receiving his. Things had really come full circle for me. I always said I would never forget the feeling I got when Tim Brown took the time to respond to my letter after I had watched him play against Michigan State. And now, the roles were reversed. It was a position I always dreamed about being in, and I felt rejuvenated and motivated to keep getting better. He wrote me that I was an inspiration to him, yet *he* had also been a source of strength when I felt things weren't going well for me.

After I sent the letter to Jonathan, I received a letter from his father:

Dear Tim:

My name is Mike. I'm from Ashley, Pennsylvania, and now live in Lancaster, Pennsylvania. My son Jonathan recently wrote to you about the passing of his grandma and his indecision on sports.

The letter you wrote in return was outstanding, motivating, and truly from the heart! You cannot believe the excitement and effects of that letter. He was truly ecstatic that you took the time to answer him. No one but you read that letter. It was hidden from me, his mom, and his brother Mike (18). Since then he rejoined the football team in winter weightlifting, signed up and started baseball practice, and is working out at home. He really came out of his shell and opened up. His grandma was really his inspiration. She attended all of his LL games from tee-ball to twelve-year-old all-stars. She also sat through all his football games despite rain, cold, and his broken bone in his wrist (he missed three games). She was his real inspiration, now you are.

I was floored by simply writing a letter I could have such a positive impact on someone. Jonathan's dad went on to say he was planning on coming to our annual spring game with his two sons, and he wanted to meet me. Unbeknownst to me, he had called Coach Davie and told him the entire story. One day, when Coach Davie had called up the team after a spring practice, he told the whole team about Jonathan. He said they would be at practice the following day and he was going to introduce them to the entire team.

The next day at practice, Coach Davie introduced Jonathan in front of the team, while his father and brother looked on. I could tell Jonathan was a little embarrassed, but I also knew he'd remember the moment for a long time. Jonathan, his brother, Mike, and his dad watched the practice, and then I sat with them at the pre-game meal that is open to the public before the annual spring game. It was an honor to learn more about Jonathan and his brother. They were Irish Catholic and "were born wearing ND clothes." After the spring game, I took Jonathan, his brother, Michael, and his dad into the Notre Dame locker room. I could tell they were very excited about the whole weekend experience, and I'm glad I had some small part in it.

Jonathan and I kept in periodic contact since that day, and two years later I received a letter from him telling me about another tragedy in his life. His girlfriend had been in a car accident and the doctors told the family she was not likely to make it. Through the power of prayer and her will to fight, she successfully emerged from the coma and is on track to live a normal life. Jonathan continues to inspire me, even years after our first encounter. He stayed by her side every night, praying and providing support. I could have never imagined at the time a simple letter could create a bond between two people. To me, this is everything Notre Dame is about. There is a spirit to Notre Dame, and it cannot be explained unless you are willing to wrap your heart and mind around it.

When the summer rolled around, I told my parents I *had* to stay at Notre Dame so I could work out and condition with my teammates. I always wondered if I I had hurt my chances of playing by going home the previous summer. Even though I knew I had worked as hard as I could, the fact was, the coaches couldn't see how hard I was working when I was out of their sight. I did not want to have any regrets, so I convinced my parents to let me stay at Notre Dame for the summer even though I'd be foregoing some much needed income my summer job back home at the steel plant would have provided. They acquiesced when I secured a job as an assistant manager at St. Edward's Hall that would pay for my room and board.

My summer schedule was a mixture of pleasure and pain. I had a tremendous amount of fun, but it was interspersed with working out extremely hard. I was able to find a healthy balance between the two extremes. I was only taking one summer class that met twice a week, so I had plenty of time to hang out by the pool, play golf, and enjoy the summer weather. But my leisure activity was coupled with working out for four hours per day. I became very close with my teammates during these weight training and conditioning sessions.

You can't help but grow closer together when you see your team-mates pushing themselves to the brink of exhaustion. I think you are able to feed off each other's energy.

I became very good friends with our starting fullback, Tommy Lopienski, that summer. He was the hardest worker I had ever met, and we often did extra running together after we'd worked out with the team. His work ethic was incredible, and he was always going above and beyond the required time commitments. He had a whole workout he would follow on his own, in addition to the required workouts we did as a team. He was the only guy the coaches ever had to tell to not work so hard because they were worried he would injure himself since he never gave his body a chance to rest. We did everything together that summer, and I highly respected his discipline and drive. Tommy was my confidante and many of our conversations revolved around football. He knew I was frustrated I was not playing, and he encouraged me to talk to one of our special teams coaches about it.

I took his advice and went to the football office to meet with the special teams coach who was in charge of running the punt block team.

He was a new coach who had just joined our program the previous spring, so he had only been acclimated to Notre Dame for a little more than six months. I felt the punt block team was where I could have the biggest impact on a game. Every day in practice I ran against our first string punt team, and I had success in blocking several kicks. My efforts in practice had not garnered me an opportunity to play in a real game, and I was frustrated with the disconnect. I was welcomed into the coach's office and when I sat down across from the coach he asked me what was on my mind.

I moved to the edge of my chair before saying, "Coach, I believe I can contribute and help this team win. I believe I've earned an opportunity to earn a starting job on the punt block team, and I'll do whatever it takes to make that happen."

I will never forget what he said to me in response. His office had a window facing the stadium, and he pointed out the window as he spoke.

"Tim," he said, "I've been hired to do a job. It is my job to put the best eleven players on that football field, and I would be doing a disservice to every Notre Dame fan if I didn't do that. I'm not just going to put a guy out there because he's a hard worker."

I do not know what his true intention was in telling me this, but I took the response as a personal assault on my abilities and a complete slap in the face. I think he thought I was asking to be given something I had not earned. I am embarrassed by what transpired next. Before I could respond, my eyes spoke louder than any words I could have spoken. There in front of my coach, three-and-a-half years of pouring my heart, soul, and mind into Notre Dame football boiled to the surface and, no matter how hard I tried to resist the feeling, I couldn't. I began to cry. The tears of frustration flowed, and the more I tried to make them stop, the harder they fell. I was embarrassed to be crying in front of my coach because I didn't want to appear weak, especially when I was trying to make my case for a spot on a special team. It was one of only a few moments in my life when I couldn't control my emotions.

When I finally composed myself after a few awkward moments I said, "Look, Coach, I wouldn't be here if I didn't think I was good enough to play on that field. I can look you straight in the eye and say I am confident I can do the job better than any guy you could put out there. I'm not asking for a chance because I'm a hard worker, I came to talk to you because I don't think I've been given a fair chance to prove myself."

I walked out of the office glad I had communicated how I felt. I wished I had not let my emotions get out of control, but at least the coach knew I was passionate about wanting to play. I was also cognizant of the fact an opportunity to play never materializes in a coach's office. Playing time is earned on the playing field and is why I was always reluctant to go and talk to a coach about giving me an opportunity to play. I always tried to let my play speak for itself. But I reached a point where I was not playing, and I thought I had done everything under my control to earn an opportunity, so I had to do something. Whether or not my meeting with the special teams coach would translate into playing time remained to be seen, but I wanted to plant the seed I was not intimidated and I felt, at the very least, I earned a chance to compete.

The only one of my teammates I told the story to was Tommy, and he laughed about as hard as a person can laugh when I told him what happened. He never let me live down the fact I cried in front of a coach.

The summer was a tremendous experience. I wouldn't say I worked harder than I did when I was back in my hometown the previous summer, but the experience of working out with my teammates was immeasurable. My arm was slowly healing, but I was not at the point I had been before my junior year. It was a long road, but I was determined to get back what I lost. Because I was unable to do as much as I wanted with my upper body, I tried to compensate by overworking my legs and abdominal muscles. Every day in the silence of my dorm room, I did one thousand sit-ups, then I placed a backpack filled with books on my lap, and performed wall sits until I fell to the ground.

My obsession with working out was perhaps best exemplified one night when I was in a movie theater in South Bend. I was sitting in the very front row of an uncrowded theater, when I began to feel guilty I was just sitting down and not doing anything to get better. So I got out of my seat and started doing sit-ups in the front of the theater. I followed a set of sit-ups with a set of push-ups before returning to my seat to view the rest of the movie. The tunnel vision I had with respect to my football goals wouldn't allow me to simply sit and enjoy the movie. Thankfully, I was sitting in the front of the theater so no one (that I know of) could see my exercise intermission.

Our summer workouts culminated in the "Wednesday Night Massacre." This was our strength coach, Mickey Marotti's, brainchild. The event was held on one of the last nights the team was together before going home for a few days to get ready for fall camp. The players were allowed to get dressed up in preparation for the final hard workout of the summer. The event was meant to add some brevity before the hard work of two-a-day practices began. I painted my face like a skeleton a la the movie *The Program*, wore army fatigues, a camouflage bandana, and a white tank top. Other fashions sported that night included *Braveheart* look-alikes wearing kilts and blue war paint, two brave souls who painted their entire bodies red, and other creative costumes appearing battle ready. If an outsider had wandered into the weight room they would have thought we were part of a gladiator casting call. It was a lot of fun. Despite being one of the toughest workouts of the summer, it brought the team closer together and culminated the summer conditioning.

I left Notre Dame to go home for a few days following a successful summer of intense training and prepared myself for fall camp. I pushed myself as hard as I knew how, and I was confident good things were in store for my senior year. This was going to be the year everything would fall into place for me. Or so I thought.

FOURTEEN

WINNERS NEVER QUIT

*"What is important is not what happens to us,
but how we respond to what happens to us."*

~ Jean-Paul Sartre, 20th-century Nobel Prize-winning,
French existentialist writer~

My senior year I reported to fall camp with high expectations. I stayed on campus all summer to work out, and I felt ready to contribute on the football field. I had my sights set on earning a job on the punt block team, but when the special teams depth chart was released, I was not on it.

During the first two days of fall camp I came the closest I ever had to quitting. I truly felt like walking out, and it was only after talking to my parents and teammates I calmed down. I knew deep in my heart I would never quit, but I was seriously questioning whether all my work had been fruitless. I did not know what else I could do to put myself in a position to play. Furthering my frustration, on the third day of fall camp, one of my ribs cracked during practice. My arm had finally healed and now I had to contend with a cracked rib. It hurt to breathe and sneezing was almost unbearable. The injury kept me sidelined for a week and a half—almost all of fall camp. It was the first time in four years I ever missed a two-a-day practice. I was able to return to practicing with the aid of a cortisone shot injected directly into my rib cage after missing the most significant portion of fall camp. *How can I prove to the coaches I deserved an opportunity to play if I'm not even practicing?* The entire summer of staying on campus and working out seemed like it had gone for naught.

I reached a tipping point. I was so frustrated with my situation, I felt I had to do something or I was in danger of losing the positive attitude I worked hard to maintain. I decided to talk to Coach Davie about my situation before practice one day. As I sat with him on the golf cart that had become his trademark mode of transportation to practice, I told him I felt I had done everything in my power to earn a spot on a special team, and I did not know what else I could do. Coach Davie was responsive, but he also knew I was still nursing a rib injury. He said once I got healthy, he would give me an opportunity. The conversation was encouraging, so I began to see a little light at the end of the tunnel. I came away from the conversation wishing I had talked to Coach Davie much sooner instead of allowing the frustration to slowly mount.

Our season started out a disaster. We started the year with three straight losses for the first time in Notre Dame's storied history. This was not the kind of legacy any of the seniors wanted to leave behind. During this tumultuous period, the press brutalized Coach Davie and questioned his ability to continue to lead the program. During this stretch, putting me on a special team was the least of Coach Davie's concerns, and my disappointment seemed to mirror our entire season.

I would not play a down the entire 2001 season en route to a 5-7 record, and I spent many nights wondering if all the work I had put into Notre Dame football had been worth it. I knew I would take away valuable lessons that would serve me later in life, but I would be lying if I said I was not disappointed in my football career. One of the philosophies I had always lived by was to work hard and have confidence in your abilities and good things will eventually happen. I had worked hard, had confidence in my abilities, but I was still waiting to see the fruits of my labor. It is extremely disappointing to face the reality that something you have always believed does not seem to be true. I felt better when I found out Santa Claus was not a real person.

When the season ended, speculation ran rampant Coach Davie was going to be fired. The nature of big-time college football comes down to one common denominator—winning. During my four-year career, we enjoyed two 9-3 seasons coupled with two 5-7 campaigns. This lack of consistency along with no national championships and no bowl victories had the Notre Dame faithful calling for our head coach's dismissal.

Every player received a phone call on the Sunday morning following the last game of our season against Purdue. I was not in my dorm room because I was sitting in the waiting area of a Pep Boys while a friend's car was being serviced, so I was unaware a team meeting had been called. As I sat in the waiting room on a hard plastic seat thumbing through some dog-eared magazine, a special report came across the wall-mounted television screen:

Bob Davie was fired today as Notre Dame's head coach after compiling a 35-25 record during his up-and-down tenure. The search for a new head coach will begin immediately.

It was a very impersonal way to have the news communicated, and I was disappointed I missed the hastily organized meeting where Coach Davie met with the team before the story became public. If I had been present at the meeting, I would have had a chance to say goodbye to my coach. As it was, in the whirlwind following his departure, I never got a chance to talk to him before he left. Coach Davie didn't leave in a bitter coup de grace and conducted himself with class until the end. Coach Davie, as the quote at the beginning of this chapter exemplifies, always preached to us life is not about the bad things that happen to us—it is how we handle them that determines our success or failure. Everyone on the team knew Coach Davie was under a tremendous amount of pressure and his job was on the line. But throughout the season, Coach Davie never allowed the pressure to consume him. He knew his every move would be questioned publicly in the media and privately behind closed administrative doors, but he never allowed that fact to affect his interactions with the players.

With the season over, and our team left without a coach, I had come to a crossroads in my football career. In the coming months I faced an important decision—should I return for a fifth year of eligibility or leave Notre Dame and begin the rest of my life? Everything in my heart was telling me to stay because I felt there was more to accomplish, and I felt I had fallen short of my goals. I knew if I chose to forego my final year of eligibility the rest of my life I would regret it. I also knew the possibility remained I would put in another year of work and again come away frustrated by not reaching my personal expectations. But if the latter scenario did come to fruition, I, at least, would never have to ask myself the painful "what if " question. I could live with failure; I couldn't live with regret.

My decision was multi-faceted because I also had to convince my parents to let me stay for another year. They had supported me for four years through financial sacrifice, and I would have to again ask for them to subsidize my education for one more semester. They had been my number one fans since I first started participating in athletics, rarely ever missing a game. I knew they believed in my abilities, but I also think they didn't want to see me sacrifice for another year and go further into debt, only to endure another disappointing season of sitting on the bench. But in my mind, I was willing to pay off loans for the rest of my life if it meant I would have one more season to play for Notre Dame.

My final decision was made easy for me during a study break, while studying for an Irish language final exam. I was sitting in my dorm room trying to conjugate Gaelic words, when my mind started to drift to what I would be doing with my life in the coming months. While trying to memorize the Gaelic language off note cards, my thoughts were broken into two very distinct pictures. As my eyes stared at the note card—*an fuinneog*=the window—I think it sent a subliminal message to my subconscious, and I looked out the window at the white snow blanketing the ground. The first picture I envisioned was of another three months of waking up at 5:45 a.m. and trudging through the snow to the Loftus Center for morning workouts. Then I recalled the training and sacrifice I faced with another summer of working out in preparation for the season, and yet another fall camp with two-a-day practices in the summer swelter.

I struggled with my focus—*Ag an bhfuinneoig*=At the window—was the last note card I fought through before placing the cards down and allowing my mind to continue to wander. For once I allowed myself to picture the next three months without football to occupy my time. It would be nice to not have time constraints and a daily schedule that left room for social activities. If I wasn't preparing for another season, I could maybe go to a movie on a random Wednesday night and stay up past midnight on a weekday. Heck, I could even order a pizza and not pick the cheese off and wash it all down with a sugary soda. As quickly as I considered the thought, I dispensed the idea because I knew every time I'd run into one of my teammates walking across campus or in the dining hall I'd miss the camaraderie. And the truth was, I still loved the discipline and work required to go through another off-season, so despite the short-lived allure of the path of least resistance, my heart wanted to remain at Notre Dame for another year. To see if my decision was in agreement with cosmos, I decided to try a little experiment.

There was a deck of cards sitting on the corner of my desk and I decided to attempt a dance with destiny. I was looking for a sign that returning for a fifth year of eligibility was going to be the right decision.

I sat in my room and asked for some guidance, *I need a sign coming back next year is what You have in store for me. I've been frustrated, but I remain positive good things are going to happen. Please show me I'm on the right track and everything will work out according to Your plan.*

To test my faith I decided to try something I had never done before. For fifteen solid minutes I rested my hand on the deck of cards and concentrated on the first card that came into my mind—the queen of hearts. I kept repeating the words "queen of hearts" inside my head and picturing the card in my mind. After fifteen minutes I shuffled the cards and fished out a card from the middle of the deck. I held it face down in my palm before slowly flipping the card over. I blinked to make sure I had seen correctly; there in my hand was the queen of hearts.

If the card would have been the four of spades, would that have affected my decision to return for a fifth year? No. But I felt something powerful compelling me to stay, and I was reassured to keep following the dream. I kept that queen of hearts to serve as a reminder to me that if I believe in something enough, I can often make it happen.

A week after firing Coach Davie, a national search resulted in the hiring of a new head coach. George O'Leary, the former head coach of Georgia Tech, was introduced to the masses during a school-wide pep rally. After O'Leary was introduced to the Notre Dame faithful, he addressed the congregation and stated his goal of returning Notre Dame to national prominence. This, of course, was met with thunderous applause as the crowd waved in the air the free "By George, it's O'Leary" t-shirts that had been handed out to all in attendance. The entire teams sat on the floor of the basketball arena and listened to our new head coach speak for the first time. I don't remember much from his inaugural press conference, but something he said the first time he addressed the team privately sticks out in my mind.

It was during a team meeting the following day when our new head coach said, "I only have one rule—don't lie to me."

The irony of this statement would become apparent in the days following that first team meeting. Four days after our first contact with our new head coach, George O'Leary resigned after admitting he lied about his academic and athletic background. He claimed to have a master's degree in education from New York University and to have earned three letters playing college football at New Hampshire, but checks into his background showed both to be untrue. So, George O'Leary, would not be the man to lead us back to national prominence. We again, found ourselves without a coach.

A few weeks later, while at home on Christmas vacation, I heard on the news we had hired Tyrone Willingham, from Stanford, to be our next head coach. I did not know much about him at the time, but I would soon find out.

FIFTEEN

LEADERSHIP

"Leaders aren't born they are made. And they are made just like anything else, through hard work.

~Vince Lombardi~

After I returned from Christmas vacation, I met the man who would have a profound impact on my life. It was during a team meeting inside Notre Dame stadium our second head coach in three weeks was first introduced to the team. His introduction came with considerably less fanfare than when Coach O'Leary was unveiled to the Notre Dame community. There was no pep rally and no free t-shirts were passed around. It was an intimate gathering of players and administrators and all eyes were focused on Coach Willingham. The team was a blank canvas, ready and willing to be painted in whatever direction our new coach wanted to direct us.

With the introductions over, Coach Willingham stoically looked at his new team from his vantage point in the front of the room, while everyone in attendance was forming first impressions. One of the managers dimmed the lights and Coach Willingham began his initial team address with the aid of a PowerPoint presentation. *Who was this guy?* I'd never had a coach use a PowerPoint presentation during a team meeting. From the moment the meeting started, it was apparent Coach Willingham was meticulously organized. The first slide he showed the team on the large screens stationed on either side of the front wall, said simply, "WIN."

The more he talked, the more I felt my own conscious was talking to me. He talked about winning in everything. Winning in the class-room. Winning in our spiritual and social development. And finally, winning on the football field. He chose his words carefully, rarely raising his voice, but his message came across loud and clear. Under Coach Willingham, nothing but one's best would be tolerated. He told us we would be a program that did not make excuses. We would be a program that would win, and win the right way. He made no provisions for a rebuilding year. Specifically, he addressed the seniors and assured us we would not be forgotten while he tried to indoctrinate the younger players into his system. We looked to him to provide leadership, and in return, he looked to us.

In doing a little research on my new head coach, I learned we had a lot in common. He had also been a walk-on during his playing days at Michigan State. The process by which he earned a spot on the Michigan State roster was similar to mine, in he had written letters to dozens of Division I schools in hopes of finding one that would give him an opportunity. I could also relate to him because he didn't have the proto-typical size of a Division I college football player either. To me all that mattered was whether or not I was a good football player, prototypical size or not. I think he felt the same way. So from my standpoint, I do not think I could have created a better coach if I were to make one up in my own imagination. Everything I gleaned about Coach Willingham from reading different articles spoke to his incredible discipline and work ethic. Coach Willingham impressed me before I ever had my first individual conversation with him.

Since I did not play as a freshman, I could return for a fifth year, if the Faculty Board of Athletics granted me another year of eligibility. This was an oversight committee charged with having the final say on all matters regarding the fifth year application process. For me to return for a fifth year, it would cost my parents and me approximately $12,000. My sister was recently engaged and all the money in our household was geared towards making the wedding arrangements. I knew my decision, not only affected me, but it also would have a monetary effect on my family. But after talking with my parents, with their blessing, I made the decision to return for a fifth year at Notre Dame.

At Notre Dame, the fifth-year process is unique. In order to return for a fifth year as an athlete, you must maintain a minimum of nine credit hours if you haven't yet graduated. If you have already graduated, you are required to take a minimum of twelve credit hours. I already had enough credits to graduate with a major in finance, so in returning for a fifth year I wanted to limit my costs as much as possible. With each credit hour costing $1,100, it behooved me to defer my graduation so I would be allowed to take fewer credits during my fifth year. I decided to declare Theology as a minor, so I would not be placed on the graduation list in May. In order to complete my minor, I needed six more theology credits in the fall semester of my fifth year. I had to find a way around Notre Dame's nine credit minimum rule, so I would be allowed to only take the six credits I needed to complete my minor.

Notre Dame is the only Division I school in the country requiring nine credits to return for a fifth year. At any other school, all you have to do in order to return for a fifth year is take the credits you need in order to graduate. So, if you only need one credit to graduate that is all you have to take during your fifth year. However, at Notre Dame you must take a minimum of nine credits, regardless of how many credits you need to graduate. This hard and fast rule did not apply to all students. Any non-athlete can return for a fifth year and take one, two, or three credits and still be enrolled in the University. Because of this, I decided to appeal the nine-credit rule to the Faculty Board on Athletics.

Coach Willingham met with all the players on an individual basis shortly after he arrived. At the time I went to speak to him, I was in the appeal process trying to be allowed to take six credits instead of nine. I spoke to him about my situation, and he said he would speak to the faculty board on my behalf. This small gesture meant a lot to me. When I went in to speak with him he did not sit behind his imposing desk and hide behind his authority. Instead, he walked around to the front of his desk and sat down in a chair next to me. We sat there talking like we were old friends. Coach Willingham looked me directly in the eyes when he was talking to me, and it was a struggle not to look away. I mustered up the courage to tell him what I had practiced many times in preparation for the meeting.

I said, "Coach, I've put on the uniform, I've run through the tunnel, and I've played in a couple of games. I realize how lucky I am to be a part of Notre Dame football, but at the same time I just want an opportunity to prove myself. I feel like the last four years the carrot has been dangled out in front of me and just when I'm about to catch it, someone snaps it away. The only reason I want to come back next year is because I feel I can help the team win, and I would like that opportunity."

He looked at me and said, "Tim, I can't promise you anything. But I can promise you that you'll have an opportunity."

That response was all I needed to hear, and I walked out of Coach Willingham's office with something to prove.

The off-season was a lot like being kicked in the head, getting back up, and then getting kicked in the head again. We had lifting and running almost every day and then on Saturday mornings, at 6:00 a.m., we had a team conditioning session. In our very first Saturday morning workout, Coach Willingham asserted he was not just going to be a figurehead in our program.

After we had station conditioning for an hour, consisting of various football related drills, all the players lined up in our stretch lines. We started clapping, and figured our work for the day was done because everyone was dripping with sweat and on the verge of exhaustion. Coach Willingham had other ideas, and clapping it up and going home wasn't one of them. He proceeded to take us through an abdominal and push-up workout that would have made the Navy Seals proud. I think he got the routine from a video called "Torture Tactics." Did he stand up in front of the team and blow his whistle and belt out instructions like every other coach I'd ever had? No. He got down and did the routine with us. Now, this was a coach we could go to war with.

At one point when the echoes of strained voices and grunts were rebounding off the walls inside of the Loftus Sports complex, our coach, our leader, said simply, "Stop whining!" That first conditioning session set the pace for the rest of the off-season, and led to many sleepless nights anticipating 6:00 a.m. Saturday morning workouts.

Unlike the off seasons in my previous four years, we were told at the end of our two and a half months of conditioning we would be having a combine exactly like the NFL combine. We would be getting tested in the forty-yard dash, the number of times we could bench press 225 pounds, vertical jump, pro-shuttle, three-cone drill, and the sixty-yard shuttle. Everything I did in the off-season was focused on impressing the coaches with my testing. It was a rare occasion when I didn't stay after a workout to work on my speed and quickness.

During the off-season I also began doing pool workouts with my teammates Tommy Lopienski, Jeff Faine, and Rocky Boiman. Tommy and Jeff had both decided to return for a fifth year, and Rocky was preparing for the NFL combine. Each pool session was under the supervision of one of the assistant strength coaches, who was constantly pushing us. My three teammates provided good motivation during these pool workouts where we'd strap weighted vests to our chests and work on our running form. Following the form running, we would go into the deep end of the pool and tread water with the weights still strapped to our chest. The water resistance provided a good change of pace from our regular workouts and the half-hour sessions were a great tool for improving our conditioning.

I felt I had given all of myself the previous four years to earn an opportunity to contribute to Notre Dame football. I had fallen short time and time again, and I knew the following season would be my last chance to come away with no regrets. I had one more year of training for a season that would potentially change my life. If I were neurotic about my training before, this year put me over the edge. I did everything I could to prove to the coaches I could play football at the Division I level. I knew I had to because of what in their eyes, was the physical liability of being only 5' 6". I threw up regularly during the off-season workouts, and the weight room became my second home. I lifted until my cheeks bulged and my body was vibrated. I often pushed myself beyond what I knew was possible, because I knew if I didn't, I had no chance of seeing the field.

It was a very rare occasion when I would ever go out to the bars with my friends. Looking back now, I think I should have forced myself to go out more, not to drink, but just to share time with my friends. After all, there's only four years to experience college. But I also felt not going out and putting myself in a situation where something could happen where I wouldn't control my own destiny was a small price to pay for the reward I felt waited at the end of the tunnel. Yes, there were days I didn't think I could take it anymore. But in return for the physical, mental, and social sacrifices, I felt there would be a fantastic, visceral payoff. That payoff would be one glorious season of Notre Dame football, where everything finally clicked.

After two and a half months, the day we had all been training for arrived. I made sure I got a solid sleep the night before the combine so I'd have no excuses when the testing arrived. The first two events I did were the pro-shuttle and the three-cone drill.

In the pro-shuttle, you straddle one of the lines on the football field and touch your hand to it. Then you start out and sprint to your right five yards, touch the line with your right hand, sprint back to your left ten yards and touch the line with your left hand, and then you sprint back through the line you started on. So, in all, you travel twenty yards.

In the three-cone drill, you start in a three-point stance and sprint five yards and touch the line before sprinting back and touching the line you started on. Then you sprint back five yards before forming a figure eight around a third cone that is perpendicular to the first, before sprinting back through the original launch point.

Both of these drills are meant to measure an athlete's quickness and change of direction ability. My times in these drills were good enough to give me one of the ten best times on the team, which meant my name would go on the "The Board." This was a plaque that hung up in the weight room and listed the top ten performers in each testing category. It was a source of pride to have your name mounted on the board and it remained there until someone beat you.

I bench pressed 225 pounds twenty-two times, which was the most among the tailbacks. My vertical was 33", second among the tailbacks, behind Julius Jones. I did twenty-eight pull-ups, which was the second most on the team behind Shane Walton, and I leg pressed the third most on the team behind Tommy Lopienski and Jeff Faine. I set personal records in every testing category, and I hoped I had proven to the coaches I was more than just a hard worker.

The same week our combine was completed, I got a letter informing me my appeal had been approved. I was going to be allowed to return for a fifth year and take only the six credits I needed to complete my Theology minor. Things were starting to look up.

The off-season workouts culminated with the combine and then we embarked on spring football practice. I was anxious to start and see how the practices would vary from the previous years. The difference could be summed up in two words: night and day. Coach Willingham and his staff had a very specific way of practicing. Little things, like running from drill to drill were emphasized, and everything we did was meant to prepare us physically and mentally for game situations. No time was wasted on running the same play twice. If a play didn't work, we moved on to the next play and waited until the film sessions to correct our mistakes. Coach Willingham knew second chances did not happen during games, so we never got a second chance in practice. The onus was on us to get it done right the first time.

If you dropped a pass, you ran to pick it up. You didn't leave it for the manager to pick up as had occurred in previous years. If a pass was dropped, or you fumbled, or you made a mental error, you had to do push-ups. Every time a skill position player touched the ball, they were required to sprint to the end zone. You didn't simply get past the secondary and then turn and run back to the huddle. You always ran to the end zone. Even if you were stopped for a one-yard gain, you would still sprint to the end zone after you got off the ground.

From my standpoint, as a walk-on, practices were even more dramatically different than they had been in years past. I used to be able to get by with only knowing a few of the running plays, because those were the only plays that would be called on the rare occasions I would get a rep in practice. Under the new regime, I had to know every-thing. All the audibles, all the passing plays, all the idiosyncrasies of the offense. I had to know not only what I did, but also what the fullback was doing and all of the receivers. I made over one hundred notecards with the plays drawn up on them, and I studied them before I went to bed at night. I can honestly say I learned more during spring practice that year than I had in the previous four. The coaches genuinely cared about developing you as a player, even if you were a walk-on fifth year senior. I shared reps with the other tailbacks during spring practice, and I was able to gain invaluable experience and confidence.

My running back coach was a man named Buzz Preston. The first time I met him we talked about my goals for the season. I told him my goal was to contribute on special teams, specifically the punt block team, and I told him I had a lot of confidence in my abilities as a running back. He told me, he too, had been a walk-on in college at the University of Hawaii. I really felt he knew where I was coming from. Coach Preston was one of the best things that happened to me. He was hard, but he was fair. He never treated me any different than any of the scholarship players. That is what I always wanted. He didn't let me accept anything but my best, and I will be forever grateful to him for the confidence he showed in me. I can also look back and laugh at the times when he would get really mad, and use such spiteful words as "Dadgummit!" and "Dagnammit!" I wanted to laugh, but he was so mad, I feared the repercussions.

After talking with Coach Preston, I spoke with the new defensive backs coach, Trent Walters, who was also in charge coordinating the punt block team. Coach Walters' son, Troy, had won the Biletnikoff Award as top receiver in college football as a 5' 7", 172-pound senior at Stanford. So, I knew it didn't matter to Coach Walters how big you were, as long as you were good enough to play. Since he was responsible for the punt block team, I expressed to him my desire to be on it. I told him I would do whatever it took to be a part of his team and all I wanted was a chance to prove myself. I started out as third string that spring on the punt block depth chart. It wasn't where I wanted to be, but it was a starting point. I had gotten on the depth chart and now it was my job to move up.

In our first scrimmage of the spring, we had two tailbacks hurt so I was able to take a lot of reps. I led the running backs in rushing with twenty-four yards on four carries. It was my first chance to carry the ball in a live situation in front of the new coaches. I think I was able to show them I could carry the ball and I was not afraid of playing against bigger players. In the second scrimmage I did not have any carries because the other tailbacks, Ryan Grant and Marcus Wilson, who were out the previous week, had gotten healthy. Our third and final scrimmage of spring practice was the Blue and Gold game, and I finished the game as the second leading rusher. I was pleased with the off-season, and I was looking forward to working out with my teammates during the summer and trying to solidify a spot on a special team.

Around the time I was in the thick of the off-season, I applied for an internship as a finance analyst at Lehman Brothers in New York City. I had an hour-long interview on campus with two vice presidents from New York. I felt the interview had gone well, but I never heard a response back from them for over a month. I had almost forgotten about the interview, and I was making plans to stay at Notre Dame over the summer so I could work out with my teammates. I received a phone call one afternoon from Lehman Brothers saying I had been offered the job. It would be a ten-week internship in New York City, and I knew it was a great opportunity to gain financial experience.

My first question to the recruiter who called wasn't, "How much is the salary?" or "How many hours will I be working?" My first question was, "Do you know of a good place to work out in New York City?"

My brother was living in New York at the time, and I would be able to live with him and save money on rent. I was lucky to have a very generous brother. The internship went from June 10 to August 16, but I started football on August 5. I told Lehman Brothers about my time commitment, and they said they would let me take the internship and only work eight weeks so I would be back in time for fall camp. I knew the internship was a tremendous opportunity for my future career, but I also really wanted to stay at Notre Dame to work out. I knew I would be working out relentlessly either way, but I thought it would improve my chances of impressing the coaches if I stayed, and deep down in the silence of my own heart I harbored hopes of getting a scholarship. I always believed if I worked hard, I should expect great things to happen and that was one goal I always held in the back of my mind from the moment I started my freshman year at Notre Dame. I was really pulled between the two decisions.

After speaking with my parents, I had little choice left. They knew what a good opportunity it was. I'd be going to New York. I explained my situation to Coach Willingham, and he told me to go. He said as long as I came back in great shape I had nothing to worry about. I told him before I left his office I would come back in the best shape of my life. I wanted him to hear that from me so if I did not, I would be letting him down. And I wasn't going to let that happen. So off to the Big Apple I went.

SIXTEEN

NEW YORK

"You come to New York to find the ambiance that will evoke your best. You do not necessarily know precisely what that might be, but you come to New York to discover it."

~Dr. James Hillman~

When I took my internship at Lehman Brothers in New York City, my oldest brother, Michael, was living on the upper west side of Manhattan on 93rd and Broadway. Luckily for me, his time in New York coincided with my internship. I moved out to New York City on Wednesday, June 5, 2002, with my good friend, and next-door neighbor, Matt Melcher. He stayed with me just for the weekend before returning home. When we arrived at New York LaGuardia airport, we told the cab driver to take us to 93rd and Broadway.

After winding through the city streets, we arrived at my brother's apartment. He lived on the top floor of a five-story building, and when we trudged up the stairs with our suitcases, my brother greeted us at the top. It was the first time I had seen his apartment, and he introduced me to his roommate. We all exchanged greetings, then I was shown my brother's room where I would be calling home for the next two months.

The first night in the city Matt, my brother, and I went out to an Italian Restaurant called Carmine's and enjoyed our first dinner in the big city. Carmine's is a popular restaurant and we had to wait for a table. While relaxing in the bar area, I noticed a familiar face. Sean Astin, the actor who played the title role in *Rudy* and Samwise Gamgee in the blockbuster hit *Lord of the Rings,* was standing less than three feet away from us. Since I was a walk-on, I felt obligated to introduce myself to the actor who had portrayed the life I was currently living.

I said, "Sean, I just wanted to introduce myself, my name is Timmy O'Neill, and I'm a walk-on at Notre Dame."

After he realized I was not some joker just trying to talk to a famous person, he could not have been more interested in talking to me. We talked for a solid fifteen minutes while we waited for our tables to be ready. It turned out Sean's wife, whom he later introduced me to, was from Indiana. He was curious to know what I thought about the movie and if my experiences were similar to how it was portrayed in the movie. It was great to hear his stories about his time filming at Notre Dame. It turned out Sean was at the restaurant for a cast party for *Lord of the Rings,* and he introduced me to many of the cast members. Sean was a class act, and he gave me his e-mail address. We've exchanged several e-mails since that night at the restaurant.

The next day, Thursday, I spent $250 on a gym membership for the summer. After crossing that off my list, my brother drove us outside of the city to Sam's Club so I could load up on some groceries. I bought seventy-two cans of tuna fish, orange juice, cereal, chicken breasts, and bagels. In my mind, I now had everything I needed: A job, a place to stay, food, and a place to work out. That afternoon, Matt, my brother, and I went to the *David Letterman Show.*

My first weekend in New York City was exciting, and it was good to be able to share it with my good friend. But, by Sunday night, my friend was gone, and I would be starting my job the next day. I bought three brand new suits for the occasion, and I laid my favorite one out and set the alarm for 6:30 a.m. I didn't have to be at work until 8:00 a.m., but I wanted to make sure I had plenty of time to get ready for my first day.

My first day on the job I was introduced to the other twenty interns in the program. They were from Columbia, Northwestern, Babson,

Emory, Georgetown, and Carnegie Mellon. There were two of us from Notre Dame—myself and Mike, whom I had never met prior to that first day. We received our assignments for the summer. My assignment was to be a finance analyst for the information technology department. I was excited for this new opportunity, and I felt welcomed immediately.

I was assigned to a desk and had two mentors who helped guide me through the internship process. My manager was the same person who interviewed me so it was reassuring to see a familiar face. Throughout the eight weeks on the job, I worked very closely with all of the people in my group. They made my time in New York very enjoyable and from that first day, they really took me under their wing. I got off work at 6:00 p.m. That is when my real work began.

As soon as I got off the job, I went directly back to my brother's apartment to change into my workout clothes. I had a strict workout I followed for the next eight weeks in preparation for the season. Mondays I did quickness drills, an upper body lift, and conditioning. Tuesdays I did a speed workout, plyometrics, and a lower body lift. Wednesdays I did distance running. Thursdays was again quickness drills, an upper body lift, and conditioning. And Fridays were the same as Tuesdays, with a speed workout, plyometrics, and a lower body lift.

I found the perfect place to work out because it was only a block away from the apartment. Since Central Park was only a few blocks away from my brother's apartment, I walked there after I finished my lifting and did the running portion of my workout. Often times there were softball games going on in all of the open areas, so I would go in the outfield and do my conditioning.

Usually, the park was closing by the time I arrived, and I'd have to hop the fence in order to get on the lawn. The park rangers kicked me out on numerous occasions because they didn't want my cleats messing up the field. I didn't know how my cleats were any different than the cleats the softball players wore, and I told them so. They, in turn, called the New York City police, and they told me I could not do my running there. So I left, waited until the police officers were gone, then I hopped the fence again to finish my running. I knew I was not doing anything wrong, and I had a football season for which to prepare.

After one of my clandestine trips to sneak onto the field, I miscalculated my timing, and the police officers could still see me hopping the fence. They quickly returned and stood by the edge of the fence and asked me to come over and speak to them. I thought I was going to get a severe tongue-lashing. When the officers asked me what I was doing, I explained to them I was preparing for a football season at Notre Dame.

The officer looked at his partner, smiled, and said, "Well, you're lucky you don't play for Michigan."

After they found out why I needed the field, they never gave me any more problems. Not only were they honorable New York City police officers, they were Notre Dame fans.

On the third day of my visit to Central Park, I saw two kids my age who were throwing a football. They were obviously training because they were running specific routes. We started talking, and I learned they were both Division III football players at Connecticut Wesleyan. Mosah was a quarterback, and John was a wide receiver. We exchanged cell phone numbers and for the rest of the summer we met in Central Park nearly every day to work on running routes and catching the football. They became my good friends, and they helped with my training immensely. I caught thousands of balls that summer from the right arm of Mosah—and dropped hundreds.

I remember one day in particular where I had to test myself in a conditioning drill. I had to run three 300-yard shuttles, which consisted of sprinting sixty yards back and forth five times. I was not looking forward to the day at all. When I got off work at 6:00 p.m., I had to run to the subway because it was pouring rain. When I finally arrived back at the apartment, my suit was soaking wet. So I took my soiled clothes off and changed into my workout clothes. I walked down the stairs and looked outside and it was still pouring rain. *Should I just do the conditioning test tomorrow instead?* What I wanted to do was go back upstairs and watch TV. But I knew that was not going to make me any better. So I went outside and made my way to Central Park. Everyone in the city was rushing to get inside a cab or get indoors. Not me. I was on my way to Central Park to do a conditioning test.

Central Park was a ghost town when I arrived and by then sheets of rain were coming down. I set up my markers sixty yards apart, and I got my stopwatch ready. I did that conditioning test and it was just me and Mother Nature who knew about it. I'll never forget that day because when I had finished my third 300-yard shuttle, I looked down at my stopwatch and I had made my times for the first time that summer. I looked up at the sky, with the rain falling down on me, and I screamed as loud as I could. It was going to take more than a little rain to detour my plans.

Meanwhile, I was learning a lot during my time at Lehman. It gave me an opportunity to learn firsthand about the inner working of an investment bank. The people I was working with were extremely talented, and I was so happy I decided to come to New York. I was having the best of both worlds. I was making money to help pay for my fifth year, and I was also able to work extremely hard in preparation for the season.

About midway through the summer, I heard from a friend of mine on the team that two of my walk-on teammates were awarded scholarships—John Crowther and Pat Dillingham. I couldn't have been happier for them. John was one of my best friends, had been our long snapper for two years, and he truly deserved it. Pat was our second string quarterback, and he had put himself in a position to be successful. I wondered if I had missed my chance at a scholarship by going to New York. I was a little discouraged, but I knew I could only control how hard I was working and everything else would fall into place if it were meant to be.

My summer in New York was very regimented. Every day I worked from 8:00 a.m. until 6:00 p.m. Following work, I'd work out until 9:00 p.m. On the weekends I threw the football with my friends in Central Park and did distance running. I had made a promise to Coach Willingham I would be in the best shape of my life when I returned for fall camp. I knew NCAA rules allowed a school to give eighty-five full scholarships. I also knew we had only given out eighty-two of those. That fact was in the back of my mind during every workout I did and every time I laced up my cleats to do the monotonous running in Central Park.

At the end of my eight weeks at Lehman Brothers, it was hard to say goodbye to the friends I had made. My department gave me a going away lunch at an Italian restaurant in the city. The day before I left, I met with the head of finance recruiting and I was offered a full-time job. I was honored. I had a tough decision to make in the coming weeks.

After I had said my goodbyes, thanked my brother and his room-mate for a fantastic two months, I was in a cab back on my way to LaGuardia. It seemed I had just arrived in the city, and I was already leaving. The summer was something I would always remember and the long nights of training were a memory I could call on when things got difficult on the practice field. As I saw the buildings recede into the background, I couldn't help feeling very satisfied with my effort that summer. Now, I had six days before I had to report for fall camp. In my mind, I was as prepared as I could have been.

SEVENTEEN

FEAR FACTOR

"Sometimes you have to go through hell
before you get to heaven."

~Anonymous~

The date finally arrived for fall camp. I was really looking forward for the season to start, even though I knew the next two weeks of my life were going to be hell. The never-ending meetings and exhausting practices definitely take their toll, both mentally and physically.

I had been in contact with one of my walk-on friends Chad DeBolt during the summer, and we both were in similar situations. We both felt we put ourselves in a position to earn a scholarship, and we looked at fall camp as the chance to prove ourselves. We had two weeks to do everything in our power to demonstrate all the work we had done during the summer. At the time of fall camp, there was a popular TV show called *Fear Factor*. The mantra greeting the contestants on the show each week was, "You have been brought here from all over the country for one reason, to stare fear in the eye as you compete for fifty thousand dollars." Every time Chad and I would see each other we would say "Fear Factor!" to remind us we were competing for a $33,000 scholarship. It was just an inside joke between the two of us, but we would say it all the time. We'd say it to each other subtlety before practice, during stretching, and at the end of practice when we were doing conditioning. It was just our little way of motivating each other during the dog days of two-a-days.

When practice started, I knew immediately things were going to be different during Coach Willingham's inaugural season. During practice I was actually getting to carry the ball and take some reps with our first string offense. Not many, but even one rep was more than I had gotten in the previous four years. My running back coach approached every practice with intensity, and he never stopped coaching me. Even though he knew I wasn't going to be the starter, he never treated me any different than anyone else. He coached everyone at my position the same, whether they were a scholarship player or not. Coach Willingham was the same way.

When the depth chart came out for special teams, I was second string on the punt block team. It was the first fall camp I had ever even been on the special team depth chart. I wanted to be first team, but hey, I had to start somewhere.

Every day of practice was one day closer to the start of the season. I knew the last day to give a scholarship was the first day of school. With each day that passed, I lost a little more hope of getting one. I kept hoping one day Coach Willingham would ask me to stay after practice so he could talk to me. It never happened. Luckily for me, Chad DeBolt kept telling me good things were going to happen. I held out hope, but the light at the end of the tunnel was starting to flicker out.

On one occasion when I got to carry the ball with the first team offense, I broke free for a long run. It happened at a time when the whole team was watching. After the run, Coach Willingham said, "Nice job." Simple, and to the point. But coming from Coach Willingham, it meant the world to me. He was never as quick to compliment me as Coach Davie, so I never really knew what he was thinking. Just to hear him say "Nice job" carried a lot of weight in my mind. The light at the end of the tunnel just got a little brighter.

After practice that day, Joe Theisman, who played quarterback at Notre Dame from 1968–1970, addressed the team. We took a knee around him, as he explained to us what it meant to be a part of Notre Dame. He came across as confident, even bordering on arrogant, but I think we needed an infusion of bravado. I remember him saying, "Notre

Dame isn't like any other university. They don't make movies about other schools. They make movies about us, like *Rudy* and *Knute Rockne, All-American*." It was just another moment for me to reflect on how lucky I was to be a part of Notre Dame football.

After about a week and a half of two-a-day practices, we moved out of our temporary residence in O'Neill Hall (no relation) and into our permanent housing. I was living off-campus for the first time, as I had spent my previous four years in Stanford Hall. We only had four more practices before school started. Time was running out. I had approached each day as if it was my last day of playing football. I had given all I had to give, and I had no regrets. Day four before school started came and went, followed by day three, day two, and day one. The night before school started, we finished practice and were having a team dinner in the press box in Notre Dame stadium. I was sitting next to Chad and, for the first time, we both didn't have anything positive to say. We knew the next day school was starting and the hope of getting a scholarship had faded into the distance.

I keep a journal. The night before school started, I wrote the most negative journal entry I had ever written. I was feeling about as low as I ever have. I wrote on Monday, August 26:

> Today it is very hard for me to stay positive. I feel like I've been trying so hard to the right thing from a physical and mental standpoint the last four and a half years, and I don't have a lot to show for it. I realize how lucky I am to be playing football at Notre Dame. But at the same time, unless you've seen the world through my eyes, you can never know how frustrating it can be. The thing that is keeping me going is knowing what I'm capable of doing if the opportunity ever presents itself. I have to believe my chance will come and when it does, I will be successful. I've worked too hard not to have something good happen this year. I really thought this was the year I would be blessed with a scholarship. I ask myself if I've done everything in my power to earn one, and my answer is yes. Dear Lord, you must have other plans for me that haven't yet materialized. Dear Lord, help me to stay positive. Please work through me to be a positive influence on others.

The first day of school, a Tuesday, I was getting my schedule straightened out so I didn't have any classes. Meetings for football started at 2:00 p.m. It was the first time I can remember I just did not feel like practicing. I got dressed and headed out to practice. I had just sat down with the other running backs and had started stretching when Coach Fillippo, the graduate assistant coach, told me I had to go back to the stadium because Coach Willingham wanted to see me. After he told me, he told another one of my walk-on teammates, Jason Halvorson, he had to see Coach Willingham also. Since practice was going to start in about fifteen minutes, we borrowed two bikes from our teammates and road them back to the stadium. Jason and I pedaled ferociously, not having any idea why Coach Willingham wanted to see us. On our way back to the stadium, I saw Chad DeBolt running out on to the practice field with a big smile on his face. He said as I raced by, "Fear Factor!" *Fear Factor?* I didn't know what he was talking about. Everything was kind of a blur.

Jason and I arrived at the stadium, threw the bikes down, and hurried inside. Coach Willingham was in his coach's office ready to go out to practice. I walked inside after knocking on the door, and he was standing there holding two pieces of paper in his hand.

He said, "I'm sorry to make you guys run back here, but I didn't think you'd mind if I asked you to sign your names on these scholarship papers."

It is hard to put into words exactly what those words meant to me. Everything stopped, and I remember every detail of the moment vividly.

Coach Willingham went on to say, "This isn't meant to be a plateau for either of you. I wouldn't have given it to you if I didn't think you deserved it. This is just the beginning, and I don't want any let ups from either of you."

I was so excited that when coach handed me the pen to sign my name on the paper, I accidentally signed my name on Jason's scholarship form. I was so happy, I think I forgot to thank him. But I think just seeing my reaction was thanks enough.

As soon as we stepped outside of Coach Willingham's office, Jason opened his arms and I jumped into them. We giggled like school children. It was a moment of pure happiness. I'm sure Coach Willingham could hear us. We went outside, let out a few more yelps, and hopped back on our bikes and went out to practice. I think I could have done anything at that moment. If you wanted me to lift up a car, I could have. If you needed me to dunk a basketball, I could have done that too.

We went out to practice, and I got back into my stretch circle like nothing had happened. The other running backs heard Coach Fillippo tell me Coach Willingham wanted to see me, so they asked me what he wanted.

I said, "I got a scholarship."

It was something I will never forget. Being able to share the moment with my teammates was very rewarding. Most of them I had sweated with for the last five years. I don't remember much about practice that day. I just couldn't wait to get back to my apartment and call my parents.

Right after practice, after I showered, I went down the tunnel and into the empty stadium. It was a moment for me to reflect on what had just happened. I climbed over the stadium wall and sat down on the bleachers listening to the beat of my own heart in the emptiness surrounding me. Flashes of everything I worked for during my time at Notre Dame came flooding back to me. All the hard times, all the good times, all the times when it would have been easy for me to give up on myself. I remembered getting out of bed and doing sit-ups when I was in high school. Running the steps of my high school stadium at midnight after dropping my friends off. Getting up at 5:30 in the morning to work out when the whole campus was sleeping. Crying myself to sleep at night when it seemed all the work was for nothing. The days of working out after spending eight hours grinding steel. Central Park. Everything came back to me. I started crying.

I pulled out my wallet and read the two quotes I had put in my wallet while waiting in a doctor's office seven years earlier. The first one was a quote by Abraham Lincoln that said, "I will prepare and someday, my time will come." The second was a quote from an article about high school athletics and it said, "Less than 1 percent of all kids playing high school athletics will ever receive any Division I scholarship." I kept those in my wallet because the one reminded me of the odds that were against me, and the other reminded me that if you keep working hard good things would happen.

When I got home I waited for both of my parents to get on the phone before saying, "Mom, Dad, I'm the newest scholarship member of the Notre Dame football team." They didn't have to say anything. I knew from their yells they got the message. It was the proudest moment of my life. They were there for me during all the frustrating times and never stopped encouraging me. Every kid should have parents like them.

The next day was Wednesday, and we were going to be opening our season against Maryland in the kick-off classic on Saturday. Our plane left Thursday afternoon. No one knew what the season would bring, but the team was confident we could beat every team on our schedule. That is the attitude Coach Willingham and the rest of the coaches brought. Only time would tell.

EIGHTEEN

4-0

"The beginning is the most important part of the work."

~Plato, The Republic~

We knew the first game was going to be critical in setting the tone for the season. Maryland had gone to the Sugar Bowl in 2001, and they were coming off a remarkable year. We needed to show the country our 2001 season was not representative of Notre Dame football.

We arrived in East Rutherford, New Jersey, on Thursday afternoon and were greeted with a welcome dinner given by the Kickoff Classic committee. Both teams attended this annual event, and we were seated on opposite ends of a banquet facility. There was no interaction with the Maryland players and the atmosphere was calm and relaxed, yet I felt an undercurrent of emotion brewing underneath the mutual respect both teams were showing. On Friday we had a walk-thru in Giants stadium, and then we went through our usual pre-game meetings on Friday night at our hotel. The meetings consist of a half hour of special teams, a half-hour of offensive and defensive meetings, and then a final half hour team meeting where game captains are announced and we watch a team highlight video. Following the team meeting, we were given a snack we carried up to our rooms to devour before getting ready for bed.

My roommate on away trips was Chris Yura, a fullback, who graduated high school as the all-time leading rusher in the state of West Virginia and, once he got to college, his bench-pressing exploits became legendary. He did the most repetitions of 225 pounds on the team with thirty-one. After the coaches came by for curfew checks, we usually had some philosophical conversations before dosing off to sleep. When my head hit the pillow in East Rutherford, New Jersey, I was praying I'd get an opportunity to play the following day.

The Kickoff Classic was a night game so we had more brief meetings Saturday morning before we were allowed to relax in our hotel room. At 5:00 p.m., we went to our pre-game Mass, which was followed by the bus trip to the stadium. Since we were the only team playing that night, all eyes in the country were watching to see how Notre Dame would react to playing a top twenty-five team under the leadership of a new coach.

Our defense played outstanding. Our offense was able to move the ball, but we could not get the ball in the end zone. Before halftime, the player who was in front of me on the punt return team, Carlos Campbell, hurt his shoulder, so I got the call to go into the game. It would be the first time I ever played in a game that had not already been decided. Since day one of joining the football team, my goal was to play in a game that mattered, and now I was getting my opportunity. It was a dream come true. My first play under the lights in Giants stadium was unremarkable. The punt was unreturnable, and, aside from the player I was blocking cordially saying, "Get off me, you little bitch!" when I continued to block him until I heard the whistle blow, it was a non-event. At halftime we led 9-0 on three field goals, and I had already almost equaled the number of plays I had played in the previous four years.

In the second half, our defense was still playing doggedly. They forced Maryland into a punting situation, and we called a middle return. I knew my job was to block the man on the end of the line, my same friend who had introduced himself earlier by asking me to get off of him. As I was blocking my man, I was trying to stay in front of him by any means necessary, and when I heard the stadium erupt I knew our punt returner, Vontez Duff, was still running. I shielded my man just enough so Vontez could make a cut, and I saw a gold blur run by me in my peripheral vision. I sprinted after him and met him in the end zone after a seventy-six-yard punt return and celebrated with my teammates. It was the biggest thrill I ever had on the football field. As I ran back to the sidelines, I couldn't resist the temptation, and I turned back and said to the Maryland player I had met earlier, "You just got blocked by a little bitch!"

We went on to win the game 22-0. At the end of the game, I heard my running back coach, Buzz Preston, call my name. There was enough time to run one more play. They called my number, and I carried the ball for a four-yard gain. I held the ball up to the stands as time expired. It was an incredible night for our football team. Despite not scoring any offensive touchdowns, our defense forced a shutout, and our kicker, Nick Setta, tied a school record with five field goals. Our cornerback, Shane Walton, also tied a school record with three interceptions. We established we were a team to be reckoned with, and I was slowly reaching my goals.

After the game, all the prognosticators that had said we were going to lose suddenly said they knew all along we would win. It was only one game, but people around the country started to take notice of Notre Dame again. The campus also started to come alive. The excitement and newness of a new head coach, combined with the first win of the season, gave the campus a tangible aura of electricity. The t-shirts made by our student government that go to support various student initiatives throughout the year evidenced this excitement. The theme for "The Shirt" in 2002 was "Return To Glory." The initial allotment of the thirty thousand green shirts sold out very quickly and more had to be ordered. Over one hundred thousand of these green shirts eventually were sold, and they helped to form a sea of green in the stands during our home games.

The following week we played Purdue. I was told during the week of practice I was going to be starting on the punt block team. It would be the first time I knew I was going to play in a game beforehand. It meant a lot to me. Just to see my name on the special team depth chart in the first team spot was very rewarding.

The night before every home game, we stayed in a hotel in downtown South Bend just to get away from the craziness of campus. I was more nervous than I had ever been before a game since high school.

When you are thrown into a game because of injury, you do not have time to be nervous. But now, I had the whole week to think about my assignment.

The game went well. Once again, our defense provided the catalyst as we scored two defensive touchdowns en route to a 24-17 victory. But, for the second week in a row, we failed to score an offensive touchdown. Again, we drove the ball well, but just couldn't get it in the end zone. I was in on six punt returns, and I did my job. It was very rewarding to be contributing on Saturdays, even if it was only on one special team. When Saturday rolled around and I was finally getting to play, it meant everything to me.

Following Purdue, our next opponent was the number six ranked team in the country, the Michigan Wolverines. Everyone was picking Michigan to dominate us, especially because we hadn't scored an offensive touchdown in two weeks. We had other ideas.

Since I had grown up in Michigan as a Notre Dame fan, this game was extra special to me. If Notre Dame happened to lose to Michigan, we'd have to take our phone off the hook because all my friends would be calling wanting to rub it in. Growing up I always carried the torch for the Fightin' Irish, even if I was outnumbered. All of my teachers knew what my goal was. All of my friends understood I could not come out and play if Notre Dame was playing on television. There was that window on Saturdays in the fall when everything just stopped. All attention and energy went into watching the Irish on television. Only during halftime did I ever go outside and throw the football. That was the ritual in the O'Neill house. Saturdays we watched the Irish.

Before the Michigan game, the legendary baseball manager, Tommy Lasorda, addressed the team. He had spoken the previous night at our pep rally, and he emotionally spoke to us again before our biggest game of the year. He had a gift for motivating. It is no coincidence why he won two World Series titles in four appearances and managed the 2000 U.S. Olympic baseball team to a gold medal in Sydney, Austrailia.

His speech must have worked because we came back into the locker room at halftime with a 16-7 lead. There was not anyone in the locker room that did not believe we were going to win. The game was sloppy, as both teams lost three fumbles and threw one interception. But in the end, we were the team that made fewer mistakes and when cornerback Shane Walton batted down a two-point conversion attempt that would have tied the game with 2:53 left, we were in a good position. But we were forced to punt and Michigan got the ball back. On Michigan's last possession, our nose tackle Cedric Hilliard pressured Michigan's quarterback into a bad pass and Shane Walton intercepted it; the entire stadium erupted, and we knew we had just written another chapter in the great Notre Dame versus Michigan rivalry.

In the locker room after the game, it was pure elation. I remember crying tears of joy because I thought back to all the times I watched Notre Dame play Michigan on TV when I was growing up, and now I was a part of it. I was having a hard time believing I wasn't dreaming. But I also knew good things had to happen because of all the work we had put in leading up to the season. Coach Willingham never got too emotional after our victories. He was satisfied with winning, but he also knew there was so much more we wanted to accomplish, and he did not want us to be happy with where we were; he wanted us to get where we were going. His attitude permeated our entire team.

The player I replaced on the punt return team had gotten healthy, so I did not play against the Wolverines. In the week leading up to the Michigan State game, I remained on second string. In my four years prior to my fifth season, I had only traveled to two away games. It was always a source of frustration for the walk-ons to practice with our teammates every day during the week, yet have to watch the game on television because we were not on the travel list. We only traveled around sixty-six players, so when the travel list came out and I was on it, it was a good feeling. It was especially sweet because I was going back to my home state and many of the kids I went to high school with would be in the stands. Many of my best friends from high school were Spartans.

We had lost to Michigan State five years in a row. It always seemed to come down to them making a big play in the waning minutes to dash our hopes of victory. The last three times we played them, they completed fourth-quarter touchdown passes to beat us. It was simply devastating. Everyone on our team remembered the feelings we had after those defeats. We were determined not to let it happen again.

On a warm and sunny Saturday afternoon in East Lansing, Michigan, we jumped out to a 14-3 lead, and we held on to that advantage until the fourth quarter. Then, Michigan State started to mount a comeback. They narrowed the lead to 14-10 and it looked like we were going to hold on for the victory. There was only 1:45 left on the clock. Michigan State faced a fourth and eleven from our twenty-one yard line. All we had to do was stop them on this play, and we were going to have our first victory over Michigan State since 1994. What happened next was perhaps the most amazing catch I have ever witnessed. Michigan State's quarterback, Jeff Smoker, scrambled and heaved the ball to the back of the end zone. It looked like the ball would sail out of bounds. That is, until their all-American wide receiver, Charles Rogers, went up and made an outstanding catch in traffic and then, with MacGyver-like ingenuity, somehow got a foot down in bounds for the touchdown.

Michigan State led 17-14. I could not believe the same scene that had played out the previous five years seemed to be happening again. This could not happen six years in a row. It was the closest thing to déjà vu I had ever experienced. The odds were stacked against us. Our starting quarterback had left the game in the third quarter due to a shoulder injury. Replacing him was Pat Dillingham, who had never even attempted a pass in a college game before getting pressed into action against the Spartans. Dillingham walked on the team as a freshman and had earned a scholarship during the summer. And for some reason I can't explain, I really believed in my heart we were going to win the game. I couldn't justify what had just happened any other way. There was no way the cosmos would let us lose six years in a row through virtually the same set of circumstances.

With around 1:30 left in the game, Dillingham hit our wide receiver Arnaz Battle on a short crossing route, and he raced sixty yards for a touchdown as our entire sideline celebrated the release of five years of frustration. Michigan State got the ball back but our free safety Gerome Sapp intercepted it on the last play of the game to secure the victory. It was one of the best games I had ever witnessed. We had waited five long years to beat Michigan state and it finally happened. Patience is bitter, but its fruit is definitely sweet.

The scene in the locker room after the game was euphoric. I am also convinced Michigan State turned off the hot water in the showers after the game because the showers were freezing. But it did not even matter because we were now 4-0 and had proven to ourselves, and the rest of the country, we could pull out the victory when the odds were against us. We needed that win psychologically more than anything else; it proved we could go into a hostile environment and win, even when there would have been every reason to give up. We would need the same resolve in the coming weeks.

NINETEEN

8-0

"It's a funny thing about life; if you refuse to accept anything but the best, you very often get it."

~W. Somerset Maugham~

oach Willingham and his staff infused a belief into our team that we could beat anyone on any day. Coach Willingham came in, refused to make excuses, and did not accept anything less than our best. And on the field, we were beginning to see the results of our work. Nothing breeds success like success, and when you start winning, it can have a snowball effect on everything you do. Unfortunately it is the same way with losing. That is why once you get into a zone, either good or bad, it is hard to pull yourself out of it. We were in a winning zone for those first four glorious weeks of the season.

I decided to turn down the job I was offered at Lehman Brothers because I had my heart set on working in sales and trading on Wall Street. The position I was offered at Lehman Brothers was a back office finance job. I wanted a job that was going to be more fast-paced, so I decided to put all of my energy into interviewing for sales and trading jobs at other Wall Street firms. It was a difficult decision to make because I really loved my time at Lehman and the people I worked with, and I was giving up a certain job in a difficult economy without any guarantees I would find another job at another firm. But if my years at Notre Dame taught me anything, they taught me to dream big and go after what I want. After speaking with a trader at Citigroup he advised me to dedicate myself to watching CNBC every day and reading the *Wall Street Journal* religiously if I hoped to land a job in sales and trading. So that is exactly what I did. I played football, and I read the *Wall Street Journal*.

Being 4-0 was a great feeling, but it would feel even better to be 5-0. Our next game was against Stanford, and it held special significance to the coaches because they spent quality years of their life in Palo Alto, California. Coach Willingham never said anything about the game being extra special to him because he had coached at Stanford, but we knew it would be an emotional game for him.

We came into the game ranked number nine in the country, but we would be without our starting quarterback, Carlyle Holiday, who was still nursing the shoulder injury he suffered against Michigan State. After his late game heroics against Michigan State, Pat Dillingham was making the first start of his career. At halftime, we trailed the Cardinal 7-3. In the third quarter, however, we scored twenty-one points in the span of 3:13 to break open a close game. The last series of the game my running back coach, Buzz Preston, sent me into the game. I waited three years for this opportunity. I had not carried the ball in Notre Dame stadium since playing Arizona State my sophomore year. On my first carry I followed my fullback Cole Laux for a seven-yard gain. I had an eleven-yard carry on the next play after a nice block from Mike Profeta. The play ended the game and it felt good to now have three carries for twenty-two yards on the season.

In my first five games of my fifth season I had already played more and traveled to more games than I had during my first four years combined. This was how I always dreamed Notre Dame football would be. I was being given the opportunity Coach Willingham promised me before I left his office after our first meeting. That is all I ever wanted.

Our next game was against a solid Pittsburgh team who came into the game with a 5-1 record. When I was growing up, the Notre Dame versus Pittsburgh game was usually a blowout, but Pittsburgh's head coach, Walt Harris, had done an excellent job rejuvenating the program. Truth be told, Pittsburgh dominated us in almost every facet of the game except the most important one—the final score. The Panthers gained 402 yards, compared to our season-low 185 yards. We had only forty yards rushing on thirty-two carries and ten first downs. But, as most of the season, we were able to get the big play when we needed it. We forced three huge turnovers and sacked Pittsburgh's quarterback eight times. We held on to the win the game 14-6 after scoring a late touchdown off a turnover in the fourth quarter. It wasn't pretty, but we found a way to win.

We were now 6-0 and people around the country who were our naysayers during the pre-season and the early part of the year began to believe. Notre Dame was the Cinderella story of the year. We were featured on the cover of *Sports Illustrated* with the caption "Return to Glory," and we had the collective eyes of the football world on us. It was very rewarding to be reaping the success of all our hard work, especially since many of us on the team endured losing seasons in the past. The electricity surrounding the football program energized the entire campus. The green t-shirts with the "Return to Glory" slogan were getting harder and harder to find, and the number one overheard topic of conversation in the dining halls and the student center was "How 'bout them Irish?" More than anything else, Coach Willingham and his staff infused a belief into our team that we could move mountains. And the week after beating Pittsburgh, we flew out to the Rockies to try and do exactly that against an undefeated Air Force team ranked number one in the country in rushing. It was a night game and was going to feature the ESPN *Gameday* crew of Kirk Herbstreit and Lee Corso. The stage was set for another great chapter in our season.

We flew out to Colorado on a Friday and got a chance to see the field and run around to help acclimate our bodies to the high altitude. I had not been playing on special teams since the Purdue game, so I probably was not going to have to deal with the altitude except during warm-ups.

By the time Saturday night rolled around, the stadium was pulsating with energy. This was the first time an undefeated Air Force team would be playing an undefeated Notre Dame team so late in the season. We were playing in front of a record crowd and seeing the student section all dressed in fatigues created a special atmosphere.

Air Force had an option attack they were executing exceptionally well coming into the game. They were leading the nation in rushing with 339 yards per game, and their quarterback, Chance Harridge, led the nation with fifteen touchdowns. During the week of practice leading up to the game, our scout offense ran hundreds of option plays to prepare the defense. Our scout team quarterback, Matt Krueger, was an option quarterback in high school so he relished the opportunity to run the option for a week. To be honest, I was a little worried headed into the game because we had done a fairly good job of running the offense during the week. Our defense had a lot of adjustments to make because defending the option is always a challenge and the defense has to play assignment football—which means if one person does not do his job, a big play usually results.

But under the bright lights of a Saturday night in Colorado Springs, our defense completely shut down the Air Force option attack. We held the number one rushing offense to 104 yards rushing. The only reason the game was close was because we turned the ball over three times. We ended up winning the game 21-14. We had completely outplayed the Falcons. Our offense had a season high 447 total yards and we had finally put together a solid game both offensively and defensively. After the game, our defense was saying our scout offense had done a better job during the week than Air Force's offense. That was a tribute to our scout team quarterback and all of the players who weren't able to travel to the Air Force game because they weren't on the travel team. Those are the unsung heroes of every football team in the country. Everyone sees the end result on Saturday on national TV, but nobody knows the preparation that went into having the opportunity to be successful in front of all those people. Many of the freshman scholarship players and the walk-ons who were watching the game back home in South Bend played a significant part in the victory. They knew their contribution even though no one else did. That is the reward and reality of being a scout team player.

We could not have been in a better situation. We were 7-0 and on our way to play the perennial powerhouse Florida State Seminoles. Florida State was coming off a last-second missed field goal that would have beaten the number one ranked Miami Hurricanes. Florida State had proven they still had the firepower despite having lost a stunner to the University of Louisville earlier in the year during a monsoon rain-like Thursday night game. We knew despite what we had accomplished up to this point in the season, there was still a whole contingent of so-called experts who were saying playing Florida State in Tallahassee would be our Waterloo. Going into the game we were double-digit underdogs and obviously the odds makers in Vegas knew this was going to be the game Notre Dame got beat. We attacked that week of practice knowing it was going to be a tremendous opportunity to prove to the country Notre Dame football was back on the national landscape.

We were riding the high of our solid performance against Air Force, and we had proven once again we could go into a hostile environment and win. When we were driving in our buses to the stadium, every Florida State fan we passed looked straight at our buses and did the tomahawk chop in an effort to intimidate us before the game even started. I loved away games. I fed off the energy of the opposing team's fans. It created a special environment that really got me excited.

We had been waiting all year to put a total team effort together—offense, defense, and special teams. We also knew we had to get off to a fast start to try and neutralize Florida State's home-field advantage. So, leading up to the game, we talked about throwing the ball deep on our first offensive play of the game. Since we scripted the first ten plays of the game, we learned on Friday night during our team meeting we were going to try and score on first play of the game on a long pass to Arnaz Battle.

We kicked off to open the game, and our defense held them to three and out. We got the ball back after a punt, and we lined up for our first offensive play of the game. I was excited because I knew what play was coming. The play was executed to perfection. Carlyle Holiday faked a handoff, rolled out of the pocket, and hit Arnaz Battle in stride, and he outraced the defense for a sixty-five-yard touchdown reception. After the touchdown, Arnaz did a tomahawk chop and then waved his arms in front of his body as if to negate the chop. It garnered him a fifteen-yard penalty, but it sent a message loud and clear—Notre Dame was not going to be intimidated.

At halftime we were tied with Florida State—10-10. But in the third quarter we exploded. Florida State stopped itself on three straight drives in the third quarter, turning the ball over three times in what proved to be the difference in the game.

On the Seminoles' second drive of the third quarter, Florida State threw an interception and we turned it into a field goal and a 13-10 lead. Two plays later, Glenn Earl hit Florida State's quarterback as he tried to scramble and caused a fumble. Ryan Grant scored on the next play, taking a pitch from Holiday and cutting back for the touchdown and a 20-10 lead. Then, to complete the glorious trifecta of turnovers, Florida State fumbled the kickoff after having it jarred loose by Carlos Pierre-Antoine, and Brandon Hoyte recovered at the Florida State seventeen-yard line. Holiday found Omar Jenkins in the corner of the end zone two plays later for a 27-10 lead. When the onslaught was over, we had scored seventeen points in just 4:23. The nail was put in the coffin when Ryan Grant broke free on a thirty-one-yard touchdown run in the fourth quarter to put us ahead 34-10.

After Ryan's run, my running back coach told me to get ready because I'd be going into the game on the next series. I was stretching on the sideline when Florida State recovered an onside kick they turned into a touchdown. Then they recovered a second onside kick and scored once more to make the score 34-24. We finally recovered the third onside kick and sealed the victory. Unfortunately I didn't get to play in Doak Walker stadium because of Florida State's late touchdowns, but it was nice to know my coach was thinking about me.

After the game the jubilation in the locker room was short-lived. We were an 8-0 football team about to be ranked in the top three in the country, and Coach Willingham was yelling at us because of how we finished the game. He was a perfectionist and he wanted us to know champions don't finish a game the way we finished our game against Florida State. But after he reprimanded us, he was dancing with the rest of us. After the game I went back out onto the field to take a picture of the scoreboard. I called home to my parents on my cell phone from the fifty-yard line after the victory. On the bus ride back to airport, the same Florida State fans who had been giving us the tomahawk chop before the game now were bowing towards the bus paying homage. Hard to believe, I know, but true. We had come into Tallahassee and humbled them. There was no better feeling in the world. And no worse feeling than the one we would all experience a week later.

TWENTY

FIRST LOSS AND LAST GAME

"When nothing seems to help, I go look at a stonecutter hammering away at a rock perhaps a hundred times without as much as a crack showing in it. Yet at the hundredth blow, it will split in two, and I know it was not that blow that did it but all that had gone before."

~Jacob Riis~

Notre Dame football was on the tongue of every sportscaster in America. The first eight games of the season could not have been scripted any better. We were under the direction of a new coach, coming off a 5-6 season, and we were now ranked number three in the latest BCS rankings. Our next three games were against Boston College, Navy, and Rutgers, and the collective sentiment was we would be 11-0 when we headed out to Southern California to take on USC in our season finale. We were playing with a tremendous amount of confidence and our practices were going well. We understood what it took to win and, heading into the Boston College game, we felt invincible.

Before the Boston College game, we warmed up in our regular blue uniforms, but when we came in from warm-ups, we had the famous green jerseys hanging in our lockers. Coach Willingham had not even told the other coaches about his intentions to have us wear the green jerseys, and the only person who knew about it was our equipment manager, Henry Scroope. As soon as we saw the jerseys hanging in our lockers, the energy in the locker room multiplied. We had all heard the famous stories of the Notre Dame teams of the past coming out in the green jerseys and now we were going to be a part of that honor. It was the first time Notre Dame had worn the green jerseys at home since 1985. But, it is never the uniform that wins the game; it's the people wearing the uniform. Unfortunately the game didn't work out how we wanted.

Everything that could go wrong did go wrong on that bitter Saturday afternoon. We fumbled the ball seven times. We lost three of those fumbles, and they were drive-killing turnovers. We also threw two interceptions, one of which was returned for a touchdown, and were a meager one of six in our red zone opportunities. Despite all our misfortune, we only lost the game 14-7. Boston College didn't so much beat us, as we handed them the game. But they did win the contest, and in the end, that is all that matters.

Complete disappointment is the only way I can describe the feelings we experienced after the loss. But the great thing about the game of football is there are so many life lessons to be learned. After a painful loss, we still had to go to practice on Sunday and do conditioning and weight lifting. There was no time to feel sorry for ourselves. While the rest of the Notre Dame family mourned, we were out on the practice field trying to atone for our sins. It is the same thing with life. After you lose your job, or you suffer a disappointment within your family or career, you have to demonstrate resiliency or you will be consumed by disappointment. A winner never feels sorry for himself. He knows the next time he will be wiser because of it, and will always let the memory stay with him so as not to repeat it. That is a unique thing about the game of college football. You only play one game a week, and you never get a chance to play the same team twice during the regular season. So, after a loss, you have an entire year to think about the feelings you had after the game—good or bad. You only have one moment in time to make your impression. You either do or you do not. On that day, Boston College beat us. We had to acknowledge and move on because we had a game to play the following week against a gritty Navy team.

Coming into the game, Navy was 1-8 and we were twenty-eight point favorites. But Navy is a team that has a lot of pride. Despite being undersized, they always seem to play their best game against us. They came out ready to play. We did not. With five minutes left in the fourth quarter, we were trailing 23-15. But we scored on a one-yard touchdown run by Rashon Powers-Neal with 4:28 left, and the ensuing two-point conversion pass to Arnaz Battle was successful to tie the game at 23-23.

I was doing a lot of praying on the sideline in Baltimore during that fourth quarter. With an answer to my prayers, Carlyle Holiday hit a wide-open Omar Jenkins for a sixty-seven-yard touchdown with 2:08 remaining to give us the victory. But more importantly, we improved our record to 9-1.

The game was also special to me because Tommy Lopienski scored his first rushing touchdown of his career. Since I had become good friends with him, I knew all of the sacrifices he had made. No one deserved to have something positive happen more than he did. His work ethic was incredible, and I was happy to see him get in the end zone—not only because of what it meant to our team, but because I knew it meant a lot to him.

After the Navy game we had a bye week before culminating our season against Rutgers. During this week, I had a final round interview in New York City for a sales and trading analyst position at Citigroup. I survived the first round interview in Chicago where I met with two managing directors. One of the managing directors was John Russell, who had graduated from Notre Dame. After speaking with him, I knew Citigroup was the opportunity I wanted. He was a class act and helped me immeasurably in the interview process. I could not have found a better mentor as I looked to begin my business career.

Fortunately, the lessons I learned through my participation in Notre Dame football translated into the interview process, and I was offered a full-time job following my New York interviews. I cancelled my other interviews and accepted the job immediately. The days of reading the *Wall Street Journal* paid dividends, and I felt fortunate to be joining a great firm. But, before embarking on my new career, I was focusing all my attention on finishing the last few weeks of my football career on a positive note.

The final home game of our season, and for most of the seniors, the final home game of their careers, was against a Rutgers team that had one win and nine losses coming into the game. Since it was my last time to put on a uniform in Notre Dame stadium, my entire family was at the game. My oldest brother, Michael, flew in from New York City, and my other brother, Patrick, flew in from Los Angeles. My sister, Mary Kate, and her fiancé, Ray Dawood, drove from Michigan with my parents. In addition, one of my best friends, J.D. Graves, and his father and brother were also there to support me in my last game. In the back of my mind, I knew I had a good chance of playing.

We took a 14-0 lead into halftime, and I was hoping we would explode in the third quarter so the guys who didn't normally get the opportunity would get to play. In the second half we did, behind the passing of Carlyle Holiday. He tied a school record with four touch-down passes, and we had a commanding 42-0 in the third quarter. It was clear Rutgers was not going to be mounting any comebacks, so the bench players began to prepare for their moment in the spotlight.

As the starters were coming out of the game, I took off my coat and started stretching. I had been standing on the sideline for nearly four hours, and it was so cold outside I could see my own breath form a cloud in the bitter air every time I exhaled. When my running back coach told me I was going to be going in the next series, I had one of my teammates cut the sleeves off the long sleeve shirt I was wearing. I did not want anything to affect my grip on the ball. While most of my teammates were bundling up inside their jackets, I was running in place to get the blood flowing again.

There was really a feeling of finality setting in for me. I knew this would be the last time I would get to carry the ball in my Notre Dame uniform. All the mornings of getting up early and lifting had come down to one last opportunity. In nearly five years I had only carried the ball five times. I had learned from those experiences the opportunity does not come very often, so when it does, you must make the most of it. It did not matter to me we were winning 42-0; all that mattered was this was my chance to prove all the work I had done was more than just getting to carry the ball in practice. I knew all of my friends would be watching the game on TV because they knew there was a good chance I was going to play. I knew my high school coach was watching, along with my four-year college roommate, the kids I went to grade school with, my relatives, my neighbors, and anyone who happened to be flipping through the channels. One of the things unique about Notre Dame is despite the fact we had a 42-0 lead, the stadium was still full, except for the small patch of Rutgers' fans that had left the stadium early in the fourth quarter.

My first play was a running play, and I got tackled after a two-yard gain. Right after the play, I was taken out of the game and we turned the ball over a couple of plays later. As I watched our defense from the sideline, I was hoping the offense would get the ball back. *Just give us one more series.* I could not have the last carry of my career be a two-yard gain. Fortunately, our defense forced a Rutgers punt with three minutes and twenty-five seconds remaining.

This was going to be my last series. The offense huddled up on the field and my running back coach called a running play off the right side of the line. I listened to our quarterback, fellow walk-on Dan Novakov, repeat the play in the huddle, and I surveyed the defense as I got into my two-point stance. I waited for his cadence and then took the ball off tackle for a five-yard gain. After the play, a Rutgers defensive linemen ripped the ball out of my hands. I was clearly down, so it was not a fumble, but I was worried the coaches might take me out of the game. *Crap!* I got back into the huddle as quickly as possible and did not look over to the sideline just in case they had any ideas of taking me out of the game.

In the huddle on the following play, Dan called "Forty-three base, on one!" It was another running play off the left side of the line. It was a zone blocking scheme, which meant I had the option to cut the play back depending on what the defensive line did after I took the handoff. My fullback was Josh Schmidt, a southern gentleman and a walk-on from Memphis, Tennessee. Even though he talked funny, he was a darn good football player, as evidenced by the fact he eventually earned a scholarship and became a valuable pass catcher out of the backfield. I lined up in the backfield again with my heels on our own seven-yard line as I surveyed the defense. I took the handoff and got a nice block from Schmidt, and then I made a cut to the left. As I turned up field, in my peripheral vision, I saw my teammate Bernard Akatu engaged in a block. I saw nothing but green grass in front of me so I just took off running. I was forced out of bounds, after what I thought was about a twenty-yard run, near our sideline. As the Rutgers defenders piled off me, my teammates and my running back coach formed a mob around me.

When I lined up in the huddle after the play I heard the announcer say, "Tim O'Neill on the carry with a forty-two-yard gain."

I finished the game with fifty-two yards on six carries, and that brought my season total to seventy-four yards on nine carries, and my career totals to seventy-eight yards on eleven carries.

After the game, I showered, and then our media director, Lisa Nelson, told me to report to the pressroom. When I entered the room a pack of five or six reporters and a TV camera surrounded me.

"Tim, did you think you were going to break that one?" a reporter from the *Chicago Tribune* asked.

"Did you know that was the longest run from scrimmage of the year?" another reporter from the *Chicago Sun-Times* asked.

Being surrounded by all these reporters, I couldn't help but thinking back to the days when I tried to enter the stadium and was told, "Sorry, son, this is for football players only."

I thought of the days I had to get dressed with the other walk-ons in the visitors' locker room. I kept answering their questions, but my mind was drifting back to the very first days of being a Notre Dame football player when the coaches did not even know my name, and I was not allowed to work out in the varsity weight room. I thought back to lighting candles at the Grotto and praying something good would happen. I thought back to the other walk-ons who had gone before me who did not get the same opportunity I did. I was grateful. I thought back to all the parties I missed because of staying home and lifting weights. I thought of all the things I had to sacrifice to be a part of Notre Dame football. I would have done it all again for the moment I experienced that day in front of my immediate family and the Notre Dame family.

The reporters eventually subsided and the camera light was turned off, but nothing could turn off the light in my heart. I learned something very valuable that day: No matter how dim the light seems to be at the end of the tunnel, you can never allow it to go out.

Following the interviews, I went out to meet my family. As was always the case after all of our home games, there was a large crowd of people outside of the players' gate. In the mass of humanity I recognized a familiar face—the father of the boy who had sent me the letter two years earlier, Mike Hart. He congratulated me and said he knew his son was at home watching the game on television.

After the game I had eleven messages on my cell phone with people checking in and congratulating me. I guess, in the end, that is why we do a lot of things in life. Just to earn the respect of our peers. I got a call from the mother of one of my best friends, and she was so happy she was almost crying. That one phone call made every morning of getting up at 5:30 worth it. Seeing the looks on the faces of my family and friends outside the locker room made me feel bad I ever, however fleetingly, thought about quitting. I hugged each and every one of them, because they knew all I had gone through during my five-year journey.

The game against USC the following week was a nightmare. They beat us, plain and simple. They were the hottest team in the country at the time, and they executed to perfection. I started the game on the punt block team, and I will always get to say I played in one of college football's biggest rivalries.

It was a disappointing ending to our season, especially with the expectations we had after our fast start. We were not selected for a Bowl Championship Series game and that was a big disappointment. We had not done what we had to do in order to solidify a spot in one of the four major bowls. We were selected to play North Carolina State in the Gator Bowl, in Jacksonville, Florida. Again, we came out flat and lost the game in a lopsided manner.

Following our loss to North Carolina State in the Gator Bowl, I sat in the locker room and reflected on my five-year journey. I didn't want to change out of my uniform because I knew I had put my gold helmet on for the last time. After fourteen years of playing football, nearly two-thirds of my life, I knew I had taken football as far as I could and my playing days were over. I watched my teammates—some crying, some putting bags of ice on bruised muscles, some in various stages of undress, some punching lockers, some cutting tape from tightly wrapped ankles, and some, like me, staring off into space. It quickly became apparent I was going to remember the losses more than the wins, the struggles more than the triumphs, and the failures more than the successes.

My memories were formed in the sweat of the off-season and in the camaraderie with my teammates. In experiencing the difficult times with them, it made me appreciate the good times that much more. So, despite the fact our national championship dreams were dashed against Boston College and we lost our final two games of the season, I realized it was only in defeat that my most valuable lessons were learned. Notre Dame football taught me if I fall down nine times I need to get up ten.

While I began to slowly untie the laces on my cleats, I felt a sadness that my football career was over. In trying to find the silver lining in the moment I reflected on how extraordinarily fortunate I was to have been a part of Notre Dame for five years. And for that, I felt privileged and honored. I tried to approach my time at Notre Dame with a certain passion because I knew I wouldn't succeed without it. As I slid my shoulder pads over my head I realized it was now time to place that passion somewhere else and begin the rest of my life.

EPILOGUE

"When you have a dream, your first and only goal should be to prepare yourself as best you can and try your best. That's all anyone can ask."

~Dan Marino~

After the season was over, I was back home in Michigan, looking through a scrapbook my mom prepared for me. While leafing through the memories, I came across a poem I had written when I was in seventh grade. It read:

Playing football at Notre Dame,
Hearing the cheers, listening to the crowd scream.
Since I was little this has
Been my dream

But this isn't a dream,
Like wishing you were a king or queen,
This is a dream that will come true,
I promise you,
Other people have done it,
So I can too.

If I work at it long and hard enough
I can be better than anyone else can be,
Because why should I let
Someone be better than me?

And as I bring this poem to a close,
Just remember the Heisman pose.

You see, when my dream started, I wanted to win the Heisman trophy. A lot of people ask if my dream was to be like Rudy. I quickly tell them I wanted to be the next Barry Sanders or Emmit Smith, never the next Rudy. Sometimes you can do everything in your power to make things happen how you want them to, and still find out in the end everything that has happened is not exactly how you imagined. But I can honestly say because I dreamed big, everything worked out better than I could have hoped. No, I didn't win the Heisman trophy, or become an all-American, but I will never wonder "what if?" I did everything in my power to make my dreams come true, and I have in my heart a reward greater than any award or honor. That reward is knowing nothing is impossible.

But if there was one lesson I learned among the many that were taught to me during my five-year journey, it is to be willing to risk everything for a dream maybe no one else can even see. Be willing to risk failure, pain, rejection, disappointment, and allowing yourself to be vulnerable to the consequences of going head first into something where the outcome is not guaranteed. I learned the measure of a man is not in what he has but in what he overcomes and learns from himself in the process. I learned to listen to my heart and to block out anything that was in contrast to the positive image I had for my future and myself. I learned how much my family, friends, teammates, and faith mean to me. I learned the only time you grow and change is when you are willing to step out of your comfort zone and risk getting your heart broken. I learned sometimes you will get your heart broken, but that is okay, because if you don't care about something enough for it to hurt when you suffer a disappointment, then you are suffering from something even worse—indifference. I learned I do not ever want to be a passive participant in my own life's journey. I learned Notre Dame will always be a part of me. And, I learned, until the day I die, I will get goose bumps when I hear the Notre Dame fight song on Saturday afternoons in the fall.

dream·er (drē'mər) *n.*

   1. A habitually impractical person.

   ~*The American Heritage Dictionary of the English Language*, Fourth
Edition © 2000 by Houghton Mifflin Company~

ABOUT THE AUTHOR

Timmy O'Neill graduated cum laude from Notre Dame with a major in finance and a minor in Theology. He currently works for Citigroup in commodity derivatives in Houston, Texas. Prior to moving to Houston, he worked in Chicago in mortgage sales and corporate bond sales and also worked in New York on the high yield and credit default swap trading desk. He is the youngest of four children, and is the fourth generation of his family to attend the University of Notre Dame.

For more information please visit: **www.everyplayeveryday.com**

Left to right: **My brother Patrick, my sister, Mary Kate, me, my mom, my brother Michael, and my dad outside the stadium after an Irish win.**

Speaking at the pep rally on the Friday night before the Stanford game.

Left to right: **Me, Minnie Mouse, and Julius Jones in Disney World two days before playing the Naval Academy in the Citrus Bowl.**

Left to right: **Me, Adam Tibble, and Matt Sarb** displaying the "walk-on" symbol at our graduation dinner.

Left to right: **Eric Nelson, me, and Tommy Lopienski** following a victory over Stanford.

Posing in the locker room after a victory. *Bottom, Left to right:* **Adam Tibble, Jeff Campbell.** *Middle:* **Eric Nelson, Brian Dierckman, Chad DeBolt, Matt Sarb, Bernard Akatu.** *Top:* **Me, Chris Mahoney.**

Jonathan Hart and me in the locker room prior to the Blue and Gold Game. After exchanging letters, we were able to meet in person.

Celebrating with my teammates after defeating Maryland in the Kickoff Classic in Giants stadium.

Celebrating in the end zone in Giants stadium following Vontez Duff's
punt return for a touchdown.

Tommy LaSorda and me in the locker room following our victory against
the #6 ranked Michigan Wolverines.

Following Jim Molinaro (70) in a game against Stanford.

2002 Notre Dame
Football Senior Class

My favorite picture: After graduation with Father Hesburgh and Father Joyce.

Playing on the punt block team vs. Purdue in my first start on special teams.

Running in the open field after a nice block from my fullback Josh Schmidt.

Saluting the crowd after a victory.